YORK NOTES

General Editors: Professor A.N. Jeffares (*University of Stirling*) & Professor Suheil Bushrui (*American University of Beirut*)

John Webster

THE DUCHESS OF MALFI

Notes by Neil King

BA (DURHAM) CERTED (CAMBRIDGE)
Senior English Master, Hymers College, Hull

  LONGMAN YORK PRESS

Acknowledgement is made to *The Guardian* for permission to reprint extracts from articles by Robin Thornber and Francesca Campbell.

YORK PRESS
Immeuble Esseily, Place Riad Solh, Beirut.

LONGMAN GROUP LIMITED
Burnt Mill,
Harlow, Essex

First published 1982
ISBN 0 582 79200 2
Printed in Hong Kong by
Wilture Enterprises (International) Ltd.

Contents

Part 1

Introduction

John Webster's life

Little is known about the life of John Webster (c.1578–c.1634). In the epistle at the beginning of his pageant *Monuments of Honour* (1624) he writes that he was born free of the Merchant Taylors' Company, and the title-page of the same work calls him a 'merchant taylor'. One John Webster was admitted to the Middle Temple on 1 August 1598 and, if the number of trial scenes and legal references in his plays is anything to go by, this may well have been our man. The first reference to his career as a playwright occurs in the diaries of Philip Henslowe (c.1555–1616) where, under the year 1602, payment is noted to John Webster and other playwrights. Henslowe managed the Admiral's Men, a company who were in direct competition with the Chamberlain's Men (later the King's Men) for whom William Shakespeare (1564–1616) wrote and to which he belonged. It is certain that most of Webster's plays were written in collaboration with other playwrights, which was a common practice then, and only *The White Devil* (1612), *The Duchess of Malfi* (1614), and *The Devil's Law Case* (c.1616) are known to have been written by him alone. The first two are enough to establish his reputation as one of the best dramatists of the English language in his or any other age, although in the Preface to the first quarto of *The White Devil* Webster mentions that the play was not well liked by the original audience. This clearly did not discourage him for long, since *The Duchess of Malfi*, his best-known play, was written soon afterwards. We do know which company performed *The White Devil*; we do know that *The Duchess of Malfi* was not written for the Admiral's Men, but for the King's Men. It was performed both in their public theatre, the Globe, and in their private indoor theatre, the Blackfriars; and we know that Richard Burbage, the actor who created many of the great Shakespearian roles, played the part of Ferdinand, and John Lowin played Bosola (Lowin was to become a remarkable veteran actor, witnessing the closing of the theatres under the Puritan influence in about 1642, and their reopening in 1660).

The Devil's Law Case has recently (1980) been revived with some success at the Theatre Royal, York; it is the first recorded production of the play since Jacobean times. Webster's achievement lies in the fact that, despite the contemporary fashion for violent, bloodthirsty plays with sensational plots, he managed to create realistic, interesting characters, avoiding the melodramatic stereotypes of many of his fellow dramatists. His plays also contain much striking imagery, and he is the best dramatic poet of his period after Shakespeare.

English drama, 1560–1642

The whole of this period of drama is sometimes referred to as 'Elizabethan Drama', and not unreasonably so, as the dramatic writing of the period gained its initial momentum under Queen Elizabeth I and, although the tone of the plays changed during the early years of the seventeenth century, the era as a whole represents the first and greatest age of English drama. Strictly speaking, Elizabethan Drama ends with the death of Queen Elizabeth I in 1603, and after the accession of James I in that year we should talk of Jacobean Drama. When he was succeeded by his son, Charles I, in 1625, the period known as Caroline Drama begins: but this is a term that is rarely used.

Elizabethan Drama

In about 1561 a play called *Gorboduc* was produced. It was significant in a number of ways: it was the first play in England that can be properly called a full-length play; it was the first English tragedy, although it adhered closely to the style of the Latin tragic playwright Seneca (4BC–AD65); it was the first play to base its story on chronicles of English history; most significantly for the development of drama in the succeeding decades, it was the first play to be written in blank verse. The authors were Thomas Norton (1532–84) and Thomas Sackville (1532–1608), both notable politicians and well-educated men, and their play marked the beginnings of drama as an increasingly popular form of literature. Travelling companies of actors had certainly for some time provided welcome entertainment in tavern courtyards and manor houses up and down the country; but now plays were becoming fashionable at the Universities of Oxford and Cambridge, the two major seats of learning, and also at court where *Gorboduc* was presented before the Queen in 1562, the first of a considerable list of recorded performances staged before her; and her liking for dramatic performance must have influenced the taste of her court.

Stage plays seem to have suited the out-going exuberance of the Elizabethans, with their love of both the refined and the earthy, their ability to enjoy a sublime madrigal and a scurrilous, obscene ballad. Many of the plays were crude in structure and written in bombastic language – a typical example is *The Life of Cambises, King of Persia*, written in the early years of Elizabeth's reign some time before 1570. The author may have been Thomas Preston (dates unknown). The overblown fustian of *Cambises* became proverbial, still being good for a joke over twenty years later in William Shakespeare's *Henry IV, Part One* (*c*.1597). A more refined play was *Supposes* (1566) by George Gascoigne (*c*.1542–78): this comedy was very successful in its time, and looks forward to the plays of the University Wits.

This is a name given to a group of men, all educated at either Oxford or Cambridge, who wrote plays for performance at their respective universities, and all of whom later worked in London during the second half of Elizabeth's reign. John Lyly (*c*.1554–1606) wrote *Endymion* (1588) and other courtly plays which did much to shape and discipline dramatic styles. He is best known, not for a play, but for his book *Euphues* (1579). It was written in a very artificial style, full of elaborate elegance, and for some years set the fashion for writing and even speaking; but by the 1590s there had been a move towards a more terse, direct style. Thomas Nashe (1567–1601), Thomas Lodge (*c*.1558–1625) and George Peele (*c*.1558–*c*.1597) – renowned for his dissipated way of living – were all playwrights of note in the circle of University Wits, but the member of the group who achieved more than any other was Christopher Marlowe (1564–93).

Marlowe is indisputably the best Elizabethan dramatist before Shakespeare. A declared atheist and a controversial figure in other ways, his major contribution to the field of drama is twofold. Firstly, he managed to breathe more life into his characters, making them more memorable by developing the rather stiff and academic structure of the plays of his time and creating greater flexibility within the accepted dramatic form. He frequently pulled the action of a play together under the influence of one dominant character, as in *Tamburlaine* (1587), *Doctor Faustus* (1588), and *The Jew of Malta* (1589), giving to the action a unity of purpose which was rare in previous plays. Marlowe's second great contribution to drama owes much to the fact that he was essentially a poet who had turned his attention to the stage; consequently he possessed the skill not merely to adopt the rather wooden and contrived blank verse, which, since *Gorboduc*, had become the accepted metre of dramatic writing, but to shape and develop it into a powerful and fitting vehicle for his dramatic language. Years later Ben Jonson (1573–1637), one of the best playwrights of the Jacobean age, was to pay tribute to what he called 'Marlowe's mighty line'. Undoubtedly the potential for some great English drama was lost when Marlowe was stabbed to death in a Deptford tavern as a result of an argument over a bill for supper and ale.

Robert Greene (*c*.1560–92) was a typical member of the University Wits. He wrote prolifically, his output including a variety of plays, works of prose romance, and many pamphlets – the most entertaining of which for the modern reader are his 'coney-catching' pamphlets, a series of essays warning against the ways of the Elizabethan underworld and cataloguing the various types of criminal. In one pamphlet, *A Groatsworth of Wit* (1592), written in a state of bitterness and poverty at the end of his life, he seems to be warning his fellow University men against an uneducated fellow, 'an upstart crow, beautified with our feathers, that . . . supposes he is as well able to bombast out a blank verse as the rest of you; and . . . is in his own conceit the only Shake-scene in a country . . .' with his 'tiger's heart wrapped in a player's hide.' This can only be a reference to William Shakespeare, an actor who had apparently decided that he could write plays as good as those in which he was currently acting.

Although Shakespeare was already in London and writing plays before Marlowe's death, his mature period of writing probably began around the year 1593, and it seems almost as if his early years were an apprenticeship for a destined role of taking up Marlowe's cloak and continuing the development and refinement of dramatic structure, characterisation and verse which Marlowe had begun. We cannot be sure of the dates of most of Shakespeare's plays as frequently we do not know when they received their first public performances, and there seemed to be no hurry to rush them into print. This was probably because Shakespeare and his contemporaries felt that plays were essentially matter to be acted – seen and heard rather than printed and read. Also, the printing of a play could be dangerous: no laws of copyright existed, and publication would facilitate the pirating and performing of your play by a rival company. We have a shrewd idea, however, of the chronological order in which Shakespeare's plays were written, and even the 'apprenticeship pieces' of the very late 1580s and early 1590s can in retrospect be seen to be among the best of their time. He experimented with Roman-style Plautine comedy, as in *The Comedy of Errors* (*c*.1589); with Roman-style Senecan revenge tragedy, as in *Titus Andronicus* (*c*.1592); with the by now traditional chronicle play, such as the three parts of *Henry VI* (*c*.1590–2); and with *Richard III* (*c*.1593) he made his contribution to the ranks of Machiavellian* megalomaniac monsters so much enjoyed by theatre-going Eliza-bethans. As confidence and control of his medium grew in the 1590s, he wrote better-balanced history plays, for example *Richard II* (1595) and the two parts of *Henry IV* (1597–8), which were much more sophisticated than the older Elizabethan chronicle plays; he wrote *Love's Labour's Lost* (*c*.1593) which, although some critics believe this to be one of his earliest plays, is startlingly inventive in its exciting use of language, and must have seemed very bright and original when first performed; and he wrote a series of exuberant comedies, including *Much*

*For Machiavelli, see p. 35.

Ado About Nothing (*c*.1598) and *As You Like It* (*c*.1599) (much of the plot of which he took from *Rosalynde* [1590] a prose romance by Thomas Lodge, who had himself taken the story from an earlier source). An original story was not considered of prime importance for a writer at this time: a prose story or play was judged by how well a tale, if it was well-known, was developed and enhanced. Another prose romance, Robert Greene's *Pandosto* (1588), was later to be taken by Shakespeare and used as a source for part of *The Winter's Tale* (*c*.1611); if Greene had still been alive he would doubtless have seen this as a bitter irony in view of his warning of some seventeen years before. With *Romeo and Juliet* (*c*.1596) came Shakespeare's first well-known tragedy. The tragic elements in the play are largely derived from the fact that the lovers are 'star-crossed', and the play does not have the power of Shakespeare's Jacobean tragedies, which tend to grow out of deep flaws and inconsistencies inside the nature of man himself – for example *King Lear* (*c*.1606). By the time Shakespeare had come to write *Twelfth Night* (*c*.1600) even his comedies have their dark side, which looks forward to the less assured spirit of the Jacobean age.

Jacobean drama

There is a noticeable change in the tone of plays written during the early years of James's reign, even by dramatists such as Shakespeare and Ben Jonson who were writing during the reigns of both Elizabeth and James.

Although a man of wide interests and a patron of the arts, King James was not an attractive figure to many of his subjects. Religious discontent was rife: the Puritan movement, out of sympathy with most entertainments and seeing playhouses as dens of vice, was gaining in strength; and ferment amongst the Catholic population was epitomised by the Gunpowder Plot of 1605, when a group of Catholics plotted to blow up the king and his entire parliament. Scientific discovery was accelerating at great pace, and for the first time men of learning began to realise that it was not possible to know everything that was worth knowing. Sir Francis Bacon (1561–1626) is one of the last representatives of a breed of men whose competence embraced literature and the arts, philosophy and science. In the same way that the confidence of nineteenth-century Victorian Britain that all things were possible has been replaced by the uncertainty and self-consciousness of the twentieth century, so the Jacobean of, say, 1610 may well have looked back with nostalgia on the closing decades of the previous century; the reign of Elizabeth may have appeared to him as halcyon days, crowned by the defeat of the Spanish Armada in 1588 by Sir Francis Drake (*c*.1540–96). Despite the fact that the last two decades of Elizabeth's reign had their troubles, the drama of the period had been, generally speaking, firm and assured: the tragedies were often bold portraits of villains who were supplanted by the forces of good in the end; the histories usually ended with consoling affirmations that a moral order and a God-ordained hierarchical society existed; and the comedies and pastoral romances were in the main sunny and carefree.

The drama of the Jacobean age was altogether more sombre. The tragedies now tended to explore corrupt worlds where human nature was rotten, and evil was not the product of a single grand villain whose expunging offered the possibility of a speedy return to a better society. The creations of playwrights such as George Chapman (*c.*1559–1634), Cyril Tourneur (*c.*1575–1626), Thomas Middleton (1580–1627), John Webster, and of the Jacobean Shakespeare are ambiguous and miasmal; and the source of the infection was often specifically sexual. The comedies of the period are rarely pastoral romances. The elegiac notes of Shakespeare's *Twelfth Night* have given way to the uncertain discords of his *Measure for Measure* (*c.*1604), and to list his *Troilus and Cressida* (*c.*1602) as a comedy, where only wars and lechery hold fashion and where a lusty boy turns into a cynic baying for bloody revenge, is indeed a sick joke. Shakespeare must have been very depressed for mankind when he wrote that play. So-called 'citizen' comedies became popular, for example Middleton's *A Chaste Maid in Cheapside* (*c.*1612), which satirised the behaviour of middle-class town-dwellers. Ben Jonson's plays *Bartholomew Fair* (1614) and *The Alchemist* (1612) are panoplies of London's teeming life; although vivid, they display the full range of human rapacity, material and sexual. Two of the harshest and most powerful satires on greed are Jonson's *Volpone* (1606) and John Marston's (*c.*1576–1634) tragi-comedy *The Malcontent* (1604).

The pleasure-loving court of the permissive King James began to increase its demand for elaborate masques and spectacles, and the emphasis on words and their poetic effect within drama began to wane. The quality of plays diminished in the 1620s, yet out of their decadence flared the occasional powerful drama such as *'Tis Pity She's a Whore* (*c.*1627) by John Ford (1586–*c.*1640). Nothing memorable was written during the 1630s, and in 1642 the public theatres were shut down by the Puritan government.

The playhouses

Before the Elizabethan age plays were performed in a variety of places: biblical plays (called Miracle plays) were staged in churchyards or market squares; there were performances of plays dealing with various vices and virtues (Morality plays) in small open-air arenas; occasionally, small professional touring companies would visit a town and be allowed to put on a play in an inn courtyard – and, if they were lucky, they might be invited to the local manor house or castle to perform an 'interlude' for the diversion of the local gentry; and rather academic comedies and tragedies, usually derived from the classical world, were performed in schools and universities. But there was no such thing as a theatre.

In 1575 James Burbage, father of the great Shakespearean actor Richard Burbage, built in Finsbury Fields to the north of the city of London the first building in England since Roman times that was specifically intended for theatrical performance. He called it, appropriately enough, 'The Theatre'. During the following decades several more open-air playhouses were built around London. The city authorities would not allow them to be built within the city, deeming them places of riot and breeding grounds for vice (theatre people themselves have never been considered quite respectable): so the theatres were sited in the fields to the north and west of the city, or behind the 'stews' (brothels) on the south bank of the Thames. These playhouses fostered a truly popular drama, and people from all strata of society, from apprentices to gallants, crowded into their yards and galleries, and even sat upon the stage itself – up to two thousand attending a single performance in some cases.

In 1599 the lease ran out on the ground upon which The Theatre stood, and the landlord refused to renew it; perhaps he hoped to cash in easily on the increasingly lucrative theatre business by capturing a playhouse when the Lord Chamberlain's Men, now headed by Richard Burbage, were forced to abandon it. If so, he was to be disappointed. Virtually overnight, the company dismantled the playhouse, carted the timbers across the river, re-erected it on the south bank, and re-named it 'The Globe' (see illustration below). This is the theatre in which *The Duchess of Malfi* and many of Shakespeare's plays were first performed. The company (themselves re-named 'The King's Men' after King James I's accession) also owned an indoor theatre at Blackfriars: this drew a more select audience. From time to time they were invited to perform at court.

There are two excellent little books which give an introduction to the playhouses of the period. They are:

BRADBURY, JIM: *Shakespeare and his Theatre*, Longman, London, 1975.
HODGES, C. WALTER: *Shakespeare's Theatre*, Oxford University Press, Oxford, 1964.

Also, the following book gives a good idea of the probable nature of the audiences:

HARBAGE, ALFRED: *Shakespeare's Audience*, Columbia University Press, New York and London, 1941.

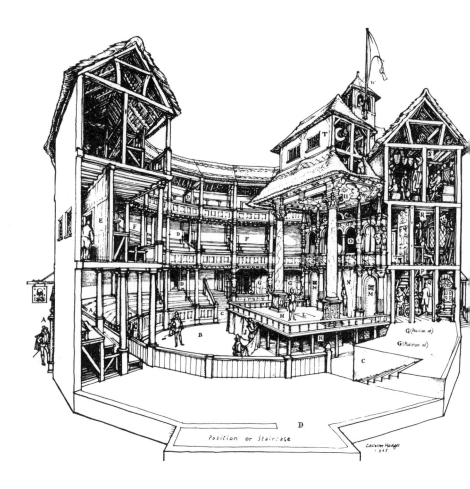

A CONJECTURAL RECONSTRUCTION OF THE INTERIOR OF THE GLOBE PLAYHOUSE

AA Main entrance
 B The Yard
CC Entrances to lowest gallery
 D Entrance to staircase and upper galleries
 E Corridor serving the different sections of the middle gallery
 F Middle gallery ('Twopenny Rooms')
 G 'Gentlemen's Rooms' or 'Lords' Rooms'
 H The stage
 J The hanging being put up round the stage
 K The 'Hell' under the stage
 L The stage trap, leading down to the Hell
MM Stage doors

 N Curtained 'place behind the stage'
 O Gallery above the stage, used as required sometimes by musicians, sometimes by spectators, and often as part of the play
 P Back-stage area (the tiring-house)
 Q Tiring-house door
 R Dressing-rooms
 S Wardrobe and storage
 T The hut housing the machine for lowering enthroned gods, etc., to the stage
 U The 'Heavens'
 W Hoisting the playhouse flag

A note on the text

During the century following the first performance of *The Duchess of Malfi* four quarto editions of the play were published. The first quarto (1623) is generally considered the best, and most modern editors use it as the basis for their editions. Research by Professor John Russell Brown has revealed that the text was probably copied out by a professional scribe, one Ralph Crane, and that his manuscript was set into print by two compositors. Apparently one compositor, in carefully (and properly) maintaining the high number of colons and semi-colons in the manuscript, used up most of the available type-sets of these punctuation marks; with the result that the other compositor, in the passages which he set up, was forced to replace many of the manuscript's colons and semi-colons with commas. The second quarto (1640) is based on the first, but contains some obvious mistakes. The third quarto (1678) corrects some of these but, as so often happens, introduces mistakes of its own. The fourth quarto (1708) is a shortened and altered version of the play, and is given the title *The Unfortunate Dutchess of Malfy or The Unnatural Brothers*; yet this quarto does contain certain sound corrections of errors occurring in previous quartos. For the best modern editions of the play see Part 5 of these Notes.

The edition of the play used in these Notes is the New Mermaids edition edited by Elizabeth M. Brennan, Benn, London, 1964, and all line references refer to that edition.

Part 2

Summaries
of THE DUCHESS OF MALFI

A general summary

Antonio, the steward of the Duchess of Malfi's household, has returned to court after a long absence in France. His friend Delio comments to him upon the various characters about the court, particularly on Bosola, a cynical malcontent who has served a seven-year sentence in the galleys for a murder which was probably instigated by the Cardinal. Yet Antonio has heard that there is goodness in this Bosola.

Ferdinand, Duke of Calabria, and his brother the Cardinal tell the Duchess that they do not wish her to marry again. Ferdinand employs Bosola to spy upon the Duchess and report to him if she receives any potential suitors. The Duchess reveals to Antonio that she loves him and secretly they go through a form of marriage. Soon Bosola suspects that the Duchess is pregnant, and her greedy devouring of a present of apricots further encourages his suspicions. When the Duchess falls into labour all her household are confined to their quarters in order to prevent discovery. The Duchess gives birth to a son. Antonio has his horoscope cast, but drops the piece of paper on which it is written. Bosola finds it, confirming his suspicions about the Duchess; yet he still does not know the identity of the father.

When Bosola's information reaches Ferdinand in Rome, the latter is enraged. He returns to Malfi and gains confirmation of Bosola's story by gaining access to the Duchess's bedchamber and confronting her. Antonio flees to Ancona and the Duchess, believing Bosola to be a friend, divulges to him that Antonio is her husband and the father of her children: which information Bosola promptly reports to Ferdinand. The Duchess and her children go to join Antonio in exile in Ancona, but they are banished from there through the intervention of the Cardinal. They consider it best to split up, Antonio heading for Milan with the eldest son. The Duchess is arrested and imprisoned by the brothers in her own palace.

Ferdinand sets about a cruel mental torture of the Duchess. By a trick she is made to believe that Antonio is dead, and she is forced to endure the company of madmen. After brief signs of despair, she bears it all stoically. Finally, Bosola supervises her strangulation, along with that of Cariola (her waiting-woman) and her children. Ferdinand immediately suffers remorse, and turns on his instrument Bosola, refusing to reward him for his services. So Bosola now plans to join with Antonio in order to gain revenge for his rejection, and he tries to use Julia, the Cardinal's mistress, in order to gain information from the Cardinal. She, however, is poisoned by the Cardinal. Ferdinand's conscience sends him mad. Antonio returns in an attempt to be reconciled with the Cardinal, gains admittance to the Cardinal's bedchamber, but in the darkness is mistaken for the Cardinal and killed by Bosola. When the Cardinal himself enters Bosola stabs him. Ferdinand enters and in his madness stabs both the Cardinal and Bosola, who manages to stab Ferdinand. All three die, leaving Antonio's friend Delio to comment on the transitory nature of powerful men and their doings.

Detailed summaries

Act I Scene 1

When the scene opens Delio is welcoming home Antonio, who has returned to the court of Malfi after some time abroad in France. Antonio explains that he likes the French court because the 'judicious' king rules well, purging the court of undesirable people and surrounding himself with good advisors.

Bosola enters, followed by the Cardinal. The Cardinal is evasive as Bosola seeks advancement at his hand for services rendered; and as Bosola states that he 'fell into the galleys' whilst in the Cardinal's employ it seems that some of that service has been of a criminal nature. Upon the Cardinal's hasty exit Bosola tells Antonio of the wealth and decadence of the Cardinal and his brother, Duke Ferdinand, who offer him nothing but promises; and he goes out muttering cynical comments about life in the court. Delio then tells Antonio that it is indeed suspected that Bosola has committed a murder on the Cardinal's behalf. Antonio recognises qualities in the neglected Bosola, but sees that 'This foul melancholy/Will poison all his goodness'.

NOTES AND GLOSSARY:
In these notes an attempt has been made to concentrate on those difficulties which, whilst they may cause trouble, are yet not so problematic that every edition of the play will have a footnote on them.

habit: dress

quits: rids

court-gall: court sore-spot. Delio implies both that Bosola is the only unpleasing sight in the court, because he lacks wealth, and that Bosola is the only man prepared to criticise the unpleasant aspects of court life

railing; rails at:	bitter mockery; mocks
galleys:	ships, usually warships, propelled by oars which were manned by criminals or slaves
dog days:	unhealthy times. The phrase is usually associated with heat, when Sirius, the 'dog star', is high in the sky. Associations with heat are frequent in this play
Tantalus:	in Greek mythology, Tantalus was condemned to thirst and hunger yet to have water and food just beyond his reach. The word 'tantalise' commemorates his tortures
the court:	Bosola's cynical comments on court life at Malfi are clearly intended to contrast with Antonio's favourable remarks on the French court earlier in this scene
suborn'd:	incited
too immoderate sleep:	excessive sleep

Act I Scene 2

The court begins to fill, and Antonio and Delio stand aside. The exact setting within the court is unspecified, although it is probably a large hall or audience chamber. Antonio promises to comment on the various characters for Delio's benefit (this is a standard way of giving information to the audience).

It seems that some court revels are in progress, and Antonio has been successful in a jousting contest. The Duke Ferdinand orders a jewel to be given to him as a prize, and then moodily expresses a wish to indulge in real warfare. There follows general conversation among the courtiers, and there is a certain amount of wit at the expense of Castruchio, an old lord whose wife, Julia, is the Cardinal's mistress.

Antonio tells Delio that the Cardinal is a court gallant on the surface, but underneath he is a 'melancholy churchman'; he is vindictive, and utilises 'flatterers, pandars, intelligencers, athiests' yet 'some good hath he done'. His brother, the Duke Ferdinand, is his 'twin in quality'. Both have no respect for the law. Yet concerning their sister, the Duchess, Antonio paints such a picture of perfect virtue that Delio accuses him of exaggeration. Cariola, the Duchess's waiting-woman, approaches Antonio and tells him that he must attend the Duchess in the gallery in half an hour.

Ferdinand recommends Bosola to the Duchess for the post of gentleman in charge of her horse, and then tells him that he is to use his position in order to spy on the Duchess and report what suitors solicit her for marriage: for she is a widow, and Ferdinand does not wish her to remarry. Bosola seems ready to cut throats, but has contempt for the status of informer; yet the Duke insinuates that it may be the way to 'a higher place', giving Bosola gold and ordering that he keep up his old reputation for melancholy, which will help act as a mask for his designs and enable him to 'gain access to private lodgings'. Bosola agrees to become the Duke's 'creature'. The Cardinal (whose name, we have learned, has already been linked with Bosola in sinister fashion) tells his brother that if Bosola is to be employed then he, the Cardinal, 'would not be seen in't'. Ferdinand says that Antonio would have been a fitter man for the job, but the Cardinal knows that he is 'too honest for such business'.

The Duke and the Cardinal tell the Duchess that they are about to depart (whence we are not told: possibly to some minor war), and combine to warn the Duchess, at some length and in menacing fashion, not to even contemplate re-marriage, for her 'perivat'st thoughts will come to light'.

When they have gone the Duchess vows that their hateful threatenings have made her the more determined to undertake a 'dangerous venture' that she has in mind. Cariola swears secrecy, and then goes behind the arras at the Duchess's bidding in order to overhear the ensuing interview with Antonio. Having called in Antonio, the Duchess asks him to prepare to write down her will, and tells him that he is to be her executor, as she has no husband; upon mention of which a brief discussion on marriage follows, Antonio claiming that never to marry is not to miss much. Suddenly the Duchess says that one of Antonio's eyes is blood-shot, and gives him her ring to apply to it, presumably as a balm: she then tells him that it was her wedding-ring, and that she vowed never to part with it except to her second husband. The implication is not lost on Antonio. She slips the ring on to his finger, saying that he deserves his fortunes to be raised. Antonio rejects ambition as 'a great man's madness', sincerely declaring his unworthiness of the Duchess. She says that she herself is the reward for his virtue, complaining of:

The misery of us, that are born great,
We are forc'd to woo, because none dare woo us . . .

and she is forced to take the initiative and kisses him. She dismisses Antonio's fears about her brothers. Cariola re-enters to witness a solemn betrothal. The Duchess then leads Antonio off, leaving Cariola to strike an ominous note by calling the Duchess's action a 'fearful madness'.

NOTES AND GLOSSARY:

the presence 'gins to fill: the audience chamber begins to fill with people; or it could mean merely that the present company is swelling

partaker of the natures of: one who has some knowledge of the characters of

took the ring: won at jousting. It is ironic that Antonio 'takes the ring' in the Duchess's jousting contest, as he will take her ring in a more literal sense before the end of this scene

chirurgeons: surgeons

jennet: small horse

shrewd turns: malicious deeds

discourse: conversation

shrifts: confessions

play the wire-drawer: exaggerate (literally, spin out)

stains: overshadows, eclipses

caroches: large coaches

cozens: tricks, deceives

intelligencer: spy, informer

candies . . . o'er: sugars over, makes appear good

politic: crafty, scheming

Laban's sheep: in the Bible, Laban was Jacob's uncle and possessed cattle, many of which were spotted or diseased (see Genesis, 30–31). Webster clearly read the Bible closely, as there are many allusions to it in the play

Vulcan's engine: this refers to the net in which in Homer's *Odyssey* Hephaestus (the Roman Vulcan) caught his wife Aphrodite (Roman Venus), with the war god Ares (Roman Mars). Webster has substituted the Roman names in this reference to Greek mythology, a not uncommon practice

chargeable: expensive

ingenious and hearty: frank and open-hearted

clew: thread to follow through a labyrinth

arras: tapestry used as a wall hanging. It served as decoration and assisted in keeping warmth in a room

tane: taken

or . . . or . . . : either . . . or . . .

affect: like

doubles with his words: makes evasive statements that can be interpreted in more than one way

I sign your *Quietus est*: when signed at the bottom of a set of accounts, this Latin phrase meant 'It is discharged' and signified that the accounts were correct. Hence the Duchess means to say that her kiss releases Antonio from his obligations to her as her steward and comes to her as an equal. Ironically, 'quietus' more commonly meant release in the sense of death: and the Duchess's kiss indeed leads eventually to Antonio's death

humorous: ill-humoured

Act II Scene 1

From the events of this scene it is clear that at least nine months have elapsed since the end of Act I.

Bosola enters in conversation with Castruchio, who wishes to be a great and respected man. Bosola gives him supercilious advice, mocking the old man. An old lady enters and Bosola turns on her, making offensive remarks about her face. She and Castruchio go out. In soliloquy Bosola divulges that the Duchess is showing every sign of pregnancy, but owing to the loose gown she wears he cannot be sure. He has brought some paricots in order to see whether she craves for them, such craving being a strong sign of pregnancy.

Antonio and Delio enter, talking confidentially. Antonio suggests to Bosola that his continued melancholy is because he would not appear puffed-up on account of his rise in status. Bosola cynically replies to the effect that princes are essentially no better than humble people: hence we can see that he is following the Duke's instructions and maintaining his reputation for melancholic cynicism.

The Duchess enters, attended by her ladies. She complains of growing fat. Bosola offers his apricots, which she greedily accepts; his suspicions are increased, but he still cannot be certain that she is pregnant. Suddenly the Duchess is taken ill, and is conveyed to her chamber. Bosola hurriedly exits. Antonio fears that she has fallen into labour before they have completed preparations for secrecy. Delio suggests it should be given out that Bosola has poisoned her with the apricots: this will give an excuse for her keeping to her apartments. Antonio is 'lost in amazement', not knowing what to do for the best.

NOTES AND GLOSSARY:

fain: eagerly

roaring boys: these were loud-mouthed bullies who were well known on the streets of Jacobean London. They liked to pick a quarrel for the sake of it, anticipating with pleasure the prospect that the ensuing argument might end in a fight

face physic: cosmetic making-up of the face

careening: scraping off paint

morphew'd: scurfy

footcloth:	ornamental cloth on a horse's back
tetter:	skin disease
lord of the ascendant:	in astronomy, the ruling planet
cousin-german:	first cousin
sound:	swoon
bett'ring of:	improvement on
farthingales:	hooped petticoats
apparently:	plainly shown
give some colour/For her keeping close:	supply a reason why she is staying in her apartments

---

Act II Scene 2

Bosola intercepts the old lady and tries to gain confirmation of the Duchess's pregnancy; but she will not listen as she fears further abuse. Antonio enters and orders all the gates to be shut. The servants rumour that a Switzer has been caught in the Duchess's bedchamber 'with a pistol in his great cod-piece'; but Antonio tells them that valuable jewels are missing and that all the officers must have their belongings searched. He sends Delio to Rome, saying 'my life lies in your service'. Delio pledges his trusted friendship, and departs. Cariola enters carrying in her arms Antonio's new-born son. Antonio immediately goes off to cast his son's horoscope.

NOTES AND GLOSSARY:

presently:	immediately
Switzer:	a Swiss, usually a member of a mercenary guard
in the Duchess' cabinet:	from the Duchess's private apartments
one o' th' black-guard:	one of the kitchen boys
set a figure for's:	cast a horoscope for his

Act II Scene 3

Despite the order confining all the officers to their quarters, Bosola is out and about in an attempt to find out more information. He thinks he has heard a woman's shriek coming from the Duchess's lodgings. Antonio enters, also having heard a noise. Meeting Bosola, he is suspicious of his purposes, and suggests that he may have given the Duchess poisoned apricots. They insult each other. Antonio declares that in the morning he will order Bosola's arrest and that until Bosola has acquitted himself it is not fit that he come anywhere near the Duchess's apartments. Aside, Antonio confesses that this deception is shameful. He departs and Bosola picks up a paper dropped by Antonio. It is the horoscope of the Duchess's son, which foretells short life and violent death. All Bosola now has to find out is the identity of the father, for he believes Antonio to be merely the go-between. He plans to send his information to the two brothers.

NOTES AND GLOSSARY:

wards:	apartments
conceit:	opinion
quit:	acquitted
bawd:	pimp, go-between

Act II Scene 4

The scene now moves to Rome. The Cardinal and Julia, his mistress, are in conversation. She is doubting his fidelity to her, and in reply he expresses cynicism towards the fidelity of women in general. He says that she owes him thanks for taking her from a generally tedious life.

A servant announces that Delio and old Castruchio have arrived in Rome. The Cardinal withdraws and Delio enters. It seems that he is an old suitor of Julia and, not knowing of her relationship with the Cardinal, proposes that she accept him as her lover. She evades him and leaves. Delio has heard that Ferdinand has received a letter that has greatly angered him, and he fears that Antonio is betrayed.

Act II Scene 5

A letter from Bosola has reached the brothers. Ferdinand is unrestrained in his language, deeming his sister 'grown a notorious strumpet' and feeling that the honour of his family is tainted. He would 'hew her to pieces'. His imagination seethes so that in his mind's eye he almost sees her 'in the shameful act of sin'. The Cardinal threatens to leave him, claiming that he is equally bitter but that 'intemperate anger' does not help. The Duke vows that he will discover 'who leaps my sister'.

NOTES AND GLOSSARY:

mandrake:	it was supposed that digging up a mandrake – a plant with a man-shaped root – led to madness
here's the cursed day:	the Duke has in his hand the baby's horoscope, which presumably Bosola has sent him
quoit the sledge:	throw the sledge-hammer
cullis:	broth

Act III Scene 1

The scene now moves back to Malfi. Antonio tells Delio that the Duchess has given birth to another son and a daughter, but he fears that her brothers know about her offspring and says that rumours are circulating among the courtiers and the common folk.

Ferdinand, the Duchess, and Bosola enter. Ferdinand says that he has arranged a husband for the Duchess, namely 'the great Count Malateste'. She rejects him as unworthy, and complains to her brother concerning the rumours about her which are circulating the court. He pretends to reject them. Left together on stage, Bosola tells the Duke that

> 'Tis rumour'd she hath had three bastards, but
> By whom, we may go read i' th' stars.

Ferdinand declares that, using a 'false key' obtained by Bosola, he will go to the Duchess's bedchamber that night and force a confession from her. He salutes Bosola as the first person he has patronised who has not been a flatterer.

NOTES AND GLOSSARY:

methinks 'twas yesterday: at least two years have passed since the end of the previous scene, and Delio's comments at the beginning of the scene are there to help the audience to accept the swift passage of time

the left-hand way: literally, in a sinister way (*sinister* being the Latin for left)

Pasquil's paper bullets: trifling satirical verses. In Elizabethan and Jacobean times it was common practice to write, and circulate anonymously, ballads attacking important people

cultures: plough-shares

gulleries: tricks

Act III Scene 2

The scene is the Duchess's bedchamber. Antonio wishes to pass the night with the Duchess. They, and Cariola, are in good spirits and there is much jesting over matters of love and beauty. While the Duchess is talking, Antonio and Cariola steal out of the room as a joke, leaving the Duchess talking to herself. Ferdinand enters unseen and overhears her talking about her children: apparently she is addressing her lover. When she turns and sees Ferdinand, he offers her a dagger in order to kill herself. She protests that she is married, if not to his liking; and asks why she should not marry – she is breaking no law or custom. He warns her (and her lover, for Ferdinand is sure that he overhears them) to hide the identity of her lover forever lest it prompt him to such violence 'As would damn us both', and can only reply to her that she is 'undone'. He tells a parable about Love, Death and Reputation in order to illustrate how she has lost the latter, and stalks out vowing 'I will never see thee more'.

Antonio and Cariola re-enter, having seen what has occurred. He turns his pistol upon her and accuses her of betrayal. She protests her innocence. There is a knock at the door, and Antonio hurries out. Bosola enters with news that the Duke 'is tane up in a whirlwind' and has ridden off to Rome, saying that the Duchess is undone. The Duchess claims that her brother was referring to the fact that Antonio has been a false treasurer and that thereby the Duke has lost money, and she bids Bosola call together her officers. While he is away, Antonio returns. The Duchess explains that he is to fly to Ancona and hire a house there, and that she will send her treasure after him. Meanwhile she must accuse him of a false crime, 'a noble lie,/'Cause it must shield our honours'.

Bosola returns with the officers, and Antonio pretends to be pleading his case to the Duchess, coincidentally echoing Bosola's complaints about ill-rewarded service. Antonio leaves, and the Duchess asks the opinions of the officers concerning him. They condemn him. When they are gone, Bosola bitterly censures them as 'lice' who hung on Antonio in his prosperity but who are quick to drop off him now. Bosola goes on to praise Antonio lavishly, so that the Duchess confides in him that Antonio is her husband. Bosola congratulates her for taking a man for his worth rather than his money or rank, promising to keep her secret. She gives him charge of all her treasure to take to Ancona, intending to follow after a few days. He pretends to advise her in friendly fashion, counselling a feigned pilgrimage to Our Lady of Loretto, and she fatally commits herself into his protection. Cariola does not like using religion as part of a deception, but the Duchess rejects this as superstition. The two women go out. Bosola declares that he will now report all to the Duke, at the same time despising himself for being an informer.

NOTES AND GLOSSARY:

with cap and knee: with cap in hand and bended knee, that is, humbly
benight the apprehension: confuse the judgment

hard-favour'd:	ugly
arras:	a sweet smelling white powder made from orris-root; not to be confused with arras, a tapestry (see p. 18)
basilisk:	a fabulous, reptilian creature whose eyes had the power to kill
Do I not dream?:	Bosola can hardly believe his luck: by saying what he sincerely thinks about Antonio's worth, and not by any stratagem, he has found out what he has been seeking for years

Act III Scene 3

Enter the Cardinal, Ferdinand, Malateste, Pascara, Silvio, and Delio.
Some inter-state warfare is in hand, and they discuss military matters.
Delio and Silvio comment aside on the effeteness and lack of real
soldierliness of Count Malateste. Bosola arrives and talks apart with
Ferdinand and the Cardinal. Those around notice threatening looks on
the faces of the two brothers who, talking apart, curse their sister. The
Cardinal says that he will persuade the rulers of Ancona to banish her
and her family. Ferdinand condemns Antonio as 'A slave, that only
smell'd of ink and counters'.

NOTES AND GLOSSARY:
guarded sumpter-cloth: decorated saddle-cloth

Act III Scene 4

Two pilgrims are visiting the shrine of Our Lady of Loretto. They
witness the Cardinal's ceremonial 'instalment' as a soldier and the
banishment (expressed dramatically in a kind of dumb-show) of
Antonio, the Duchess and their children by the state of Ancona through
the Cardinal. During this a 'ditty is sung to very solemn music, by divers
churchmen'. All depart. The two pilgrims comment on the strangeness
of so great a lady marrying so humble a person; on the Cardinal's cruelty
in wrenching the Duchess's wedding ring from her finger; on how the
Pope has seized the Duchess's state of Malfi into the protection of the
Church; and on the injustice of all these matters.

NOTES AND GLOSSARY:
This scene was omitted in the Fourth Quarto. Webster disclaimed
responsibility for the ditty; but the conversation between the two
pilgrims, which gives the audience information that the dumb-show
cannot adequately express, is generally in Webster's style.
determine of: come to a judgement about

Act III Scene 5

Antonio, the Duchess, their children, Cariola, and some servants enter,
banished from Ancona. Bosola enters with a message of reconciliation
from the Duke, and a letter asking for Antonio to be sent to him, for he
wants 'his head in a business'. The double meaning of this phrase is not
lost on the Duchess, and she tells Bosola that this show of love is a trick.
Antonio refuses to go. Bosola, contrary to his earlier comments, mocks
Antonio's lack of breeding, and exits. The Duchess suspects 'some
ambush', and persuades Antonio to flee to Milan with their elder boy so

that they cannot all be captured together. Antonio departs, fearing that they will never see each other again.

Bosola re-enters (masked so that the Duchess will not immediately recognise him) with armed men. He says that her brothers mean well towards her and that she is to be escorted to her palace; but she knows that she is in a net. He urges her to forget 'this base, low fellow'; she tells a parable of a salmon and a dog-fish in order to illustrate the difference between the worth of men in the eyes of the world and their worth in the eyes of God.

NOTES AND GLOSSARY:
right the fashion: just the way
politic equivocation: clever double meaning
this poor remainder: the few supporters who remain loyal
bottom: well or hold of a boat
scourge-stick: whip for spinning a child's top
counterfeit face: refers to (1) Bosola's mask, (2) his trickery

---

Act IV Scene 1

The scene moves to a place of imprisonment, presumably the palace at Malfi. Bosola tells Ferdinand that the Duchess is behaving nobly in adversity. Ferdinand curses her and departs.

Bosola draws a curtain revealing the Duchess, Cariola, and servants. He tells her that her brother will visit her in darkness as he has vowed never to look on her again. The servants depart with the lights and Ferdinand re-enters. He pretends to be honourable in his revenge, pardoning where he may kill. He offers her his hand as a token of peace, but to her horror she finds that she has taken a dead man's hand. Another curtain is drawn revealing 'the artificial figures of Antonio and his children; appearing as if they were dead'. All the Duchess wishes now is to die herself in any way and as quickly as possible. Ferdinand tells Bosola that the figures are 'but fram'd in wax'. Even Bosola wonders at the Duke's methods of attempting to bring his sister to despair, and suggests that he should go no further in his cruelty, but merely make her wear the dress worn by penitential adultresses. Ferdinand curses and rages over the fact that she has, as he sees it, stained the honour of his family blood. He tells Bosola that he will shortly send him to Milan to further his revenge against Antonio.

NOTES AND GLOSSARY:
directly: plainly
Portia, I'll kindle thy coals again: Portia, the wife of the Brutus who killed
                                 Julius Caesar, committed suicide by putting hot
                                 coals in her mouth, thus choking to death

remove forth: bring from
by my intelligence: by my action as informer against her

Act IV Scene 2

In order to distress the Duchess further, Ferdinand has arranged for a 'wild consort of madmen' to be lodged adjacent to her prison; but she says that the sounds of greater grief will lessen hers. Cariola thinks that the two of them will outlive this adversity, but the Duchess knows better; yet she is determined to bear her sorrow bravely, and tells the servant, who comes to tell her that the Duke has sent the madmen as a cure for her, to admit them, 'For I am chain'd to endure all your tyranny'.

The madmen enter, sing a dismal song, chatter in their various madnesses, and then dance. Bosola enters, disguised as an old man, and says that he is a tomb-maker come to make the Duchess's tomb. He emphasises her desperate situation through many images of imprisonment, decay and death. She defiantly asserts 'I am Duchess of Malfi still', attempts to be 'a little merry', and enquires of what stuff her tomb is to be made. Bosola comments on the ironic nature of the effigies of princes on their tombs.

Executioners enter with a coffin, cords, and a bell. Bosola sings a song and rings the bell, which signifies the death-knell of the Duchess. Cariola shouts and struggles and is forced off-stage. The Duchess calls after her to remember to give her little boy some syrup for his cold and to ensure that her girl says her prayers before she goes to sleep. She accepts imminent death without fear, telling her executioners to 'Pull, and pull strongly' and kneeling in order to enter heaven humbly. They strangle her. Cariola is brought back, and she tries every means to delay her death, finally claiming that she is pregnant. Nonetheless she, too, is strangled and her body removed.

Ferdinand enters, and Bosola shows him the dead Duchess and her children, also strangled, asking whether the Duke has no pity for little ones. Ferdinand feels no remorse for them, but he begins to do so for his sister, saying that if Bosola had disobeyed his orders and taken her to some sanctuary he would have been 'an excellent/Honest man'. Ferdinand protests that he was not of sound mind when he asked Bosola to kill the Duchess, reflects that he had no reason to oppose the humble nature of her marriage, yet confesses that he had hoped to gain 'an infinite mass of treasure' had she died a widow. He rejects Bosola and declares that his only reward will be a pardon for the murder. Bosola complains that the Duke himself condemned her; Ferdinand replies that no legal judgment was passed against her. Bosola claims his pension, crying out against the ingratitude of the Duke and his brother and avouching that he has served them loyally even when he hated what he was asked to do; but Ferdinand merely calls him a villain, says that he wishes never to see him again, and exits in a distracted state.

The Duchess revives for a moment and Bosola desperately tries to preserve the life in her, but she finally expires, leaving him in tears and repenting for what he has done. He determines to go to Milan in order to carry out some action fitting his depressed state.

NOTES AND GLOSSARY:

consort:	usually means a group of musicians who play or sing together, but here merely means a group or collection
hind'red transportation:	prevented from exporting
broker:	pawnbroker
perspective:	telescope
glass-house:	glass factory
lay the law:	interpret the law
placket:	opening in a petticoat
possets:	drinks of hot milk, with wine or ale and spices added
costive:	constipated
insensible:	not noticeable
salvatory:	ointment box
cruded:	curdled
puff-paste:	puff-pastry
resolve:	explain to
charnel:	charnel-house, where the bones of the dead were deposited
reversion:	inheritance
mandragora:	the mandrake root, from which the Elizabethans derived a kind of narcotic (also see notes on Act II Scene 5)
approv'd:	demonstrated
doth take much in blood:	runs in families
atonement:	reconciliation

Act V Scene 1

The scene is Milan. Antonio tells Delio that he hopes to be reconciled with the Duke and the Cardinal: but Delio suspects that letters of safe-conduct from them were to draw Antonio into a trap. He relates how the Marquis of Pescara has been made to seize back lands granted to Antonio.

Pescara himself enters and Delio, in order to find out what is happening to Antonio's land, begs that he be granted a citadel formerly held by Antonio. Pescara declines, but immediately grants the same citadel to Julia. When Delio complains, he condemns the seizure of Antonio's land which has been engineered by the Cardinal, and explains that it is fitting that such goods be given to a strumpet, and not to his friend Delio. He also tells that the Duke has come to Milan, and is suffering from some mental illness. He leaves. Antonio tells Delio that he means to gain admittance to the Cardinal's bedchamber in the middle of the night in order to try for a reconcilement; such a bold action will determine his affairs one way or the other. Delio pledges his full support in all dangers.

NOTES AND GLOSSARY:

repair: journey
in cheat: this referred to land held under a lord: if the holder committed any crime, then the property could revert to its original overlord
fraight: fraught, filled

Act V Scene 2

A doctor tells Pescara that the Duke is suffering from lycanthropia, and has been encountered at night digging up dead bodies.

The Cardinal and Malateste enter, accompanying Ferdinand, who falls upon his shadow in an attempt to throttle it. The doctor is convinced that he can control his patient, but Ferdinand throws him to the ground and beats him. Bosola, in the background, comments on the fatal judgment that has fallen upon Ferdinand. The Cardinal invents a story to account for the Duke's 'strange distraction'. Bosola comes forward, and the Cardinal enquires after the Duchess, pretending that he had no part in commissioning Bosola to kill her. He promises to reward Bosola if he will kill Antonio in order to free the Duchess for a worthy match that he has in mind. Left alone, Bosola muses on the cunning of the Cardinal.

Julia enters and announces to Bosola that she loves (or rather, lusts after) him; he plans to use her in order to find out what lies in the Cardinal's secret thoughts. He hides when the Cardinal returns; and after much persuasion the Cardinal reveals to Julia his part in the Duchess's murder, making Julia kiss the Bible in order to swear her to secrecy. The Bible is poisoned and Julia dies. Bosola springs from his hiding place and confronts the Cardinal, who again promises him fortune and honours if he will kill Antonio. Bosola reacts cynically to these promises, but agrees to do the deed. The Cardinal makes a show of the trust he places in Bosola by giving him a master key to his apartment, and leaves. Left alone, Bosola examines the precariousness of his position. He will indeed seek out Antonio, but in order to protect him from the brothers and maybe to join him in his revenge. Remorse for the Duchess haunts him.

NOTES AND GLOSSARY:

lycanthropia:	wolf-madness
Paracelsus:	Bombastus Paracelsus (1493–1541), a famous Swiss physician
present:	immediate
brook:	tolerate
fetch a frisk:	cut a caper, a light dance with jumping, frisking steps
throughly:	thoroughly, absolutely
want compliment:	do not use elegant flattering language
main ground:	principal cause
cabinet:	closet, private room
secretary:	confidante
adamant:	a substance of extreme hardness, usually referring to the diamond
frost-nail'd:	with nails in the soles of their boots in order to grip on icy ground
president:	precedent
security:	the Elizabethans tended to use this word to mean a state of feeling secure as opposed to actually being secure. Hence the word here means a complacent assurance of welfare (which leads to carelessness); it is used in the same sense in Act III Scene 5 of Shakespeare's *Macbeth* (1606)

Act V Scene 3

Delio and Antonio are outside the Cardinal's castle, which is built in the ruins of an old abbey. The place is famous for its echo. As they speak the echo reflects part of their talk. To Antonio, it sounds like the voice of his wife, and seems to speak of death and to tell him that he will never more see her. Despite warnings from Delio and, as it seems to Delio, from the echo, Antonio determines to go to the Cardinal.

Act V Scene 4

The Cardinal warns all the courtiers not to attend the Duke that night, nor to be roused by any noise that he makes during the night. They agree and withdraw. Alone, the Cardinal says that after Bosola has assisted with the disposal of Julia's body, he will die. Bosola overhears this. The Cardinal withdraws. A servant brings Antonio into the Cardinal's chamber. In the darkness, Bosola strikes down Antonio, thinking it is the Cardinal. When he realises his mistake, he tells Antonio that the Duchess and his children are dead in order to break his heart the quicker. Antonio dies, wishing that his elder son may 'fly the courts of princes'.

NOTES AND GLOSSARY:

osier:	willow
desert:	what we deserve
dark lanthorn:	a lantern with a slide or other device by which the light can be concealed
banded:	bandied
ask thee:	ask you to do
tender:	value, care for
misprision:	mistake

Act V Scene 5

The Cardinal enters, reading about hell-fire in a book. Bosola enters with Antonio's body and tells the Cardinal that he means to kill him. He rejects an offer of money. The Cardinal cries out for help; but the courtiers, who enter above, think that it is the Cardinal testing them in their promise not to come whatever the noise. The. The cries continue and Pescara decides to go down and force open the doors. Bosola kills the servant to prevent his unbarring the door. Ferdinand enters and, thinking in his madness that the Cardinal and Bosola are his enemies in battle, he deals them both mortal blows. Bosola manages to strike at, and kill, Ferdinand. Pescara and the courtiers gain entry and, before he dies, Bosola explains what has happened. Delio enters with Antonio's elder son and concludes the play by commenting on the transitoriness of greatness.

NOTES AND GLOSSARY:

Enter Pescara . . ., above:	This refers to the gallery above the rear of the stage which seems to have been common to most outdoor playhouses of the period (see the conjectural reconstruction of the interior of the Globe Playhouse on page 12; letter 'O' thereon indicates position of gallery)
come at:	come to, gain access to
engines:	tools, instruments
vaunt-guard:	vanguard
bin:	been

Part 3

Commentary

Revenge: historical and social background

In Anglo-Saxon England, if one man killed another it was considered justice for a relation of the murdered man to kill the original murderer. The problem with this kind of justice, was that frequently a relative of the original murderer now felt, rightly or wrongly, that it was a duty to avenge his own kinsman. So began a blood-feud which could go on until nearly all members of both families were dead. The feud could be ended at any time after the original murder by the payment of 'wergeld'. This word literally meant 'man-compensation' or 'man-satisfaction' and was, in effect, blood money: the murderer or his family paid the aggrieved family a sum of money which was considered appropriate for the loss of the dead man, and thus any possibility of revenge was bought off. Today we would judge this to be a very crude way of seeing justice done, but in times when there was little law and few ways of enforcing such laws as existed, the code of personal revenge was natural.

During the Middle Ages, and then the Tudor period (1485–1603), a legal system was gradually constructed which provided a formal way of dealing with murder. It came to be accepted that vengeance taken by an individual was wrong, and symptomatic of a chaotic, anarchic society; and that if any avenging was to be done, then society would do it – and would call it not revenge, but justice. If society failed to bring the criminal to justice for any reason, then it was considered that any individual who wished to see the offender punished should not take the law into his own hands, but should leave the said offender to God's justice (see the Bible, Romans 12:19: 'Vengeance is mine: I will repay; saith the Lord'). This attitude also applied to duelling: it may have been considered an honourable way for a gentleman to confront one who had wronged him, but by Elizabethan times it was increasingly considered to be another way of taking the law into one's own hands, and as reprehensible as taking revenge by means of a stab in the back, or poison. The most concise statement on revenge in the time of John Webster is Sir Francis Bacon's essay *Of Revenge* (1612). As well as being a philosopher, statesman, scientist and writer, Bacon was also a lawyer, having served at one time and another as Solicitor General and Attorney General, so his essay may be said to be a valid reflection of both the moral and legal standpoints of the time:

Revenge is a kind of wild justice; which the more a man's nature runs to, the more ought law to weed it out. For as for the first wrong, it doth but offend the law; but the revenge of that wrong putteth the law out of office. Certainly, in taking revenge, a man is but even with his enemy; but in passing it over, he is superior; for it is a prince's part to pardon. And Salomon, I am sure, saith: 'It is the glory of a man to pass by an offence.' That which is past is gone, and irrevocable; and wise men have enough to do with things present and to come: therefore they do but trifle with themselves, that labour in past matters . . . The most tolerable sort of revenge is for those wrongs which there is no law to remedy; but then let a man take heed the revenge be such as there is no law to punish . . . Some, when they take revenge, are desirous the party should know whence it cometh: this is the more generous. For the delight seemeth to be not so much in doing the hurt as in making the party repent: but base and crafty cowards are like the arrow that flieth in the dark . . . This is certain, that a man that studieth revenge keeps his own wounds green, which otherwise would heal and do well . . .

Revenge plays

Plays in which revenge is a major theme are as popular today as they were in Elizabethan and Jacobean times. This is evident from the number of television dramas where a character wishes to redress a grievous wrong done to him and, finding that for one reason or another he cannot obtain justice within the law, he takes the law into his own hands.

Elizabethan and Jacobean playwrights saw in this kind of play the opportunity to exploit a tension in their audience: if the potential avenger had been wronged, and was not merely a bloodthirsty villain himself, then the audience would sympathise with his plight and wish to see his revenge satisfied; morally, however, they could not condone revenge whatever the circumstances (see 'Revenge: historical and social background', p.31). Hence the spectator viewed the play with a mixture of dramatic anticipation and moral doubt. The usual resolution was to allow the revenger to gain his revenge, only to die himself in the catastrophe.

The earliest revenge plays of the Elizabethan period tended to be translations or imitations of the Roman plays of Seneca. They were by and large devoid of subtlety of characterisation, plot or language, relying on startling coincidences and ultimate violence and bloodshed for their effect. *Gorboduc* is a good example of an early revenge play. *The Spanish Tragedy* (*c*.1588) by Thomas Kyd (*c*.1557–94) set the pattern for revenge plays for some time, being the most popular tragedy of the

1590s. Its formula became almost a blueprint for succeeding revenge tragedies: a ghost appears who wishes to see vengeance exacted on his behalf; the main character, Hieronimo, seeks legal redress for the murder of his son but, failing to find it, vows personal vengeance; his subsequent behaviour ranges between melancholy malcontentedness and madness; he contemplates suicide; his drive for revenge corrupts his character; eventually he gains his revenge, killing his enemies but dying himself. Shakespeare's *Hamlet* (*c.*1601) contains similar motifs, and marks the beginning of a period during which some very powerful revenge plays were written, such as Chapman's *Bussy D'Ambois* (*c.*1604), Tourneur's *The Revenger's Tragedy* (*c.*1607), Webster's *The White Devil* and *The Duchess of Malfi*, and Middleton's *Women Beware Women* (1623). The occasional play appeared, for example Tourneur's *The Atheist's Tragedy* (*c.*1611), in which the hero, sometimes after hesitation, leaves revenge to heaven: whereupon heaven obliges, and the potential revenger survives. Such plays were morally more acceptable but dramatically less exciting. A curious variation on the theme is *A Woman Killed With Kindness* (1603) by Thomas Heywood (*c.*1573–1641), where Frankford treats his erring wife with such forbearance and Christian 'kindness' that she, riddled with remorse, pines away and dies. As the drama of the period degenerated generally, so the worst aspects of earlier revenge plays reasserted themselves. The last good play of the period which contains a strong revenge motif is Ford's *'Tis Pity She's a Whore*.

For ideas on how *The Duchess of Malfi* may be viewed as a revenge play see question 2 of 'Guidelines for answers' in Part 4 of these Notes.

Webster's world

One of the most difficult problems for a student of *The Duchess of Malfi* is to accept that Webster creates a possible world. It is not one to which the twentieth-century spectator or reader can easily relate, with its dark, prison-like rigidity and strict social hierarchy on the one hand, and its anarchic amorality and sudden, ruthless barbarity on the other. Would two brothers persecute their sister to the point of having her killed because she married beneath her? We tend to feel that this may have happened in some obscure seventeenth-century Italian world, and that the story is all very tragic: but that it could not happen in our world.

It is only when we begin to believe in the characters and their actions, however, that the tragedy becomes properly accessible to us. Today the audience's main reaction to the play is probably one of terror. Webster's audience most likely reacted with pity, and wept. The violence of Webster's criminals does not mean that they are totally insensitive villains: this can be seen from the reactions of both Ferdinand in *The*

Duchess of Malfi and Flamineo in *The White Devil*, when they have viewed the results of their actions. Good performances of these plays should draw us into the life of the court, making us feel that all manner of powerful forces are at work. This was certainly so in a production in Manchester, England, in September 1980, of *The Duchess of Malfi*, of which Robin Thornber (in *The Guardian*, 18 September 1980) wrote:

Marrying beneath yourself is not the sort of thing, these days, that would get you murdered by your brothers, even if they had got their eyes on your property. The achievement of this production . . . is that it succeeds in creating a world where these things matter. I mean, quite honestly, even if I was Duke of Calabria and my brother was a Cardinal, I don't think I'd be quite so gruesome about it if my sister fell for one of the staff . . . I suppose I'd learn to live with it. But no, not here in this twitching world of Webster's where everything is enhanced and heightened to a morbid degree . . . it actually seems not only credible but natural, inevitable that people should carry on in this bizarre way.

Some of the promptings of Ferdinand and the Cardinal would not be out of place in areas of modern Italy. Francesca Campbell wrote in *The Guardian* in 1966:

Murder for honour flourishes mainly in Italy's hot-blooded South where the family is still paramount and a man's good name is his most cherished possession . . . Every month one or more of these crimes are reported in the national dailies. Although often barbarous, murder for honour is not sordid: it is based on mistaken but not ignoble motives. For instance, there is the girl in a southern village who dishonoured her husband and family by committing adultery. Her father and brothers appointed themselves her executioners, asserting their prior right over the husband. She ran up the village street looking for help, but every door was barred in her face. At the top of the street they caught her and killed her. In this melodrama one finds all the basic components of an authentic *delitto d'onore*: the dishonour to the family name vindicated by the blood of the culprit, the tacit approval of the neighbours shown by their refusal to interfere, above all the taking of life from a sense of duty rather than hatred. 'Doing one's duty often hurts one's heart', as another brother said after murdering his favourite sister with a pitchfork on finding her in the hayloft with a man.

In Webster's own day, Thomas Nashe wrote in *The Unfortunate Traveller* (1593): 'The Neopolitan carrieth the bloodiest mind, and is the most secret fleering murderer.' In the light of this we can see why Webster felt that the south of Italy was an apt setting for his play.

The Italian setting

George Gascoigne's play *Supposes* started the fashion for Italian settings, and after his time many plays, both comedies and tragedies, were set there. The reasons were several. To the Elizabethans, Italy meant all that was foreign, exotic, mysterious. It was idealised as a place of sun, love and beauty – but it was also condemned as one of intrigue, violence and sudden death. It was considered that the southern heat engendered luxury and lust. Anything could happen in such a highly-charged atmosphere. Two names were mainly responsible for contemporary English attitudes: Machiavelli and Borgia. Machiavelli had written *The Prince* (1517) for the Duke of Medici, ruler of Florence. It was a bible of 'realpolitik', illustrating the politics necessary for a prince to maintain and exercise power. The words 'policy' and 'politician', used several times by Bosola in *The Duchess of Malfi*, came to mean scheming, cunning craft, and the practitioner thereof. Most of Machiavelli's precepts were followed in any European court, but the fact that he had committed them to paper unjustly made the word 'machiavellian' a dirty one, and helped to give Italy its reputation for cynical wickedness. Added to this, a series of intrigues and poisonings perpetrated by the Borgia family and others stimulated the idea of an Italy where stealthy poisoners and stiletto-in-the-back murderers operated in a way which the English gentleman felt was alien to the English spirit of dealing with matters of honour in an open fashion. If revenge was to be sought, they felt that it should be done through a challenge to a duel, or other direct confrontation, rather than by any underhand method such as poisoning a picture (*The White Devil*), a skull (*The Revenger's Tragedy*) or a Bible (*The Duchess of Malfi*), so that the intended victim may kiss it and die horribly. Also, their Roman Catholicism made Italians virtual atheists in the eyes of many an Englishman, who felt that he was morally good and socially stable. The Italian was inferior on all counts – except culturally. Their attitude was like that of the Victorians towards Cleopatra's behaviour: exotic and fascinating it may be, but so unlike the domestic life of our Queen!

The Italian setting also gave playwrights the freedom to treat at one remove matters too controversial to be given an English setting. Ben Jonson had spent some months in prison for a play called *The Isle of Dogs* (1597), which he co-authored; the little island in the Thames was too easily seen to represent England.

Women, marriage, and widowhood

Women were seen as inferior to men. They counted on the same level as a gentleman's other possessions, such as his hawks: in Shakespeare's *The Taming of the Shrew* (c.1594), Petruchio explains that he is using the methods of falconry in order to wear down his wife (see Act IV Scene 1); in Kyd's *The Spanish Tragedy*, Bel-Imperia is seen as a haughty lover who in time will stoop to lure (see Act II Scene 1); and in *The Duchess of Malfi* the Cardinal suggests that his mistress owes him thanks for his patronage in terms which describe a falconer who has shown favour to a choice falcon (II.4.27–30).

Heads of families disposed of female relatives in marriage in order to extend family honour and fortune. Sexual union was for procreation; romantic love and desire were all very well, but they were irrelevant as grounds for marriage. In the light of this it is not strange that Ferdinand should treat his sister as a possession; and it is noteworthy that in Act III Scene 1 the Duchess seems to object, not to the idea that her brother should bespeak her a husband, but only to his choice of Malateste (III.1.39ff).

As regards widowhood, here are some words which are attributed to Webster himself:

> A virtuous widow is the palm tree, that thrives not after the supplanting of her husband ... She hath laid his dead body in the worthiest monument that can be ... she hath buried it in her own heart. To conclude, she is a Relic, that without any superstition in the world, though she will not be kissed, yet may be reverenced.

Webster's sources and borrowings

Webster based *The Duchess of Malfi* on a true story. In 1490 Giovanna d'Aragona was married, aged twelve. When she was nineteen or twenty her first husband died, and some years later she secretly married Antonio Bologna, of reputable family but beneath her socially. The marriage was kept secret for years, but eventually her brothers, Lodovico (Webster's Cardinal) and Carlo (Ferdinand) found out. She and her two youngest children were taken to her palace at Amalfi and never heard of again. There is no evidence to implicate her brothers in her murder, assuming that was her fate. Some time later Antonio was murdered by a Lombard captain, one Daniele da Bozolo.

Many versions of the story were written during the sixteenth century. In the introduction to Bandello's (1485–1561) version, included in his *Novelle* (1554), he condemns revenge for the sake of honour. Belleforest (1530–83), in his *Histoires Tragiques* (1565) condemns the Duchess as a wanton, while allowing that her brothers were cruel; and several other versions see her as little better than a whore. Webster's most likely source was William Painter's (*c.*1540–94) *Second Tome of the Palace of Pleasure* (1567).

Painter's version of the story is printed as an appendix to John Russell

Brown's edition of *The Duchess of Malfi*, Methuen, London, 1964. This edition demonstrates how much Webster borrowed ideas, and even phrases, from other authors; for example, for the prison scene he used the climax of *Arcadia* (*c.*1580) by Sir Philip Sidney (1554–86), where two princes are tormented with waxen shows of one another's death. But to comment on his borrowing is not to criticise adversely: in common with many writers, Webster almost certainly kept a notebook in which he jotted down the words of others that impressed him, with the intention of using the words later himself in appropriate contexts. It was interpretation, not originality, which mattered.

The Dramatic Unities and structure

Three rules for dramatic structure had been derived from the writings of the Greek philosopher Aristotle (384–322BC). They were: Unity of Action, which stated that a play should consist of a single united action, with no sub-plots; Unity of Time, which stated that the action of a play should not last more than about twenty-four hours; and Unity of Place, which stated that the action should all happen in the same place. The French dramatists of the sixteenth century adhered closely to these rules, considering that to break them would confuse the audience and make it more difficult for them to suspend their disbelief. A good example of an English play of the period which observes the unities is Ben Jonson's *The Alchemist* (1610); but Shakespeare displays no regard for the rules in the structure of his plots, and neither does Webster. In *The Duchess of Malfi* the Unity of Action is more or less preserved: the Julia scenes may be regarded as sub-plot, but they have a bearing on the main story (see note on Julia under *Characters*). There is no regard for the Unity of Time. The Duchess's advanced state of pregnancy tells us that at least nine months have elapsed between Act I and II; and she has had three children by Act III Scene 2 (see line 280). Some critics have found it absurd that Bosola takes years to discover what an average detective might do in a day, but this is to miss the point: dramatic time and real time are not the same thing, and Bosola's policy is credible in dramatic terms. By the end of the play Antonio's son has grown to be 'a pretty gentleman' (V.5.107), suggesting that some years more have passed since Act III Scene 2 (has Webster forgotten that this is apparently the same child for whom short life and violent death were foretold in Act II Scene 3?). Unity of Place is also disregarded, and it is sometimes unclear where some scenes take place: perhaps it is just this impression of murky ambiguity that Webster wants. All of Act I occurs in the Duchess's court at Amalfi, as does Act II up to the end of Scene 3. Act II Scenes 4 and 5 take place in Rome. Act III Scenes 1 and 2 are set in Amalfi. Act III Scene 3 is set in an indeterminate place, as is Scene 5.

Scene 4 is apparently set near the shrine of Our Lady of Loretto, but it also contains a dumb-show importing the symbolic banishment of the Duchess and her family from Ancona. The whole of Act IV takes place in the Duchess's palace at Amalfi, now transformed from the place of revelry at the beginning of Act I to a place of dark imprisonment. Act V seems to take place in Milan, although this is by no means clear.

The truth is that the rules of Dramatic Unity do not matter in this play, if indeed they ever matter. Webster may be guilty of some careless craftsmanship in constructing his plot (an accusation often levelled against Shakespeare); but *The Duchess of Malfi* is an impressionistic piece, where atmosphere is conveyed through the imagery of language, and the uncertainty of place and time gives a universality to the tragedy – whether Webster intended this effect or not.

Irony

Irony is a term used to describe words which are charged with a layer of meaning different from the literal one; the subtler interpretation of which the hearer may or may not be aware. The least subtle form of irony is blatant sarcasm. More specifically, dramatic irony is a term used to describe a situation in which the speaker is unaware of the significance of what he is saying. The audience, however, is or will soon become aware of the irony. In comedy, this gives rise to mirth; in tragedy, to pain.

In Part 4 of these Notes ('Guidelines for answers', question 16) you will find a consideration of some of the irony in *The Duchess of Malfi*.

Verse and prose

Most of the play is written in blank verse, the standard medium of drama of the period. Blank verse usually implies unrhymed iambic pentameter, that is, lines composed of five stressed syllables. Usually there were ten syllables to the line, but not always: over-strictness could lead to monotony or even a comic effect, as in some of the earlier Elizabethan dramas. Sometimes there are extra syllables, or short lines for emphasis. Likewise, rhyme could be used for emphasis, or to signify ceremony, impending climax or the end of a scene.

Prose was sometimes used as a contrast: for instance, a scene of heightened passion may have been written in verse, to be followed by a low-key scene in prose. Scenes of comedy, wit and madness were among those normally rendered in prose. Hence you should notice that Bosola, with his cynical wit, speaks most of the prose in the play; and that prose is also employed for the witty exchanges of the madmen. In the conversation between the Duchess and Bosola after the dance of the madmen, the Duchess speaks mainly verse, Bosola prose; but the brevity of some of the speeches makes it unclear, and verse and prose melt into one another in a way that suggests the crisis of identity which the Duchess is experiencing (see IV.2.115–53). It also shows that both character and subject matter could affect the playwright's choice of verse or prose.

Characters

The world in which the play is set is infected, and those who are not decadent or corrupt at heart are either in some way tainted during the course of the action (see below: *The Duchess* and *Antonio*) or are in too weak a position to alter the course of events (for example Pescara in Act V Scene 1). Webster has taken from accounts of a true story the names and certain general details of characters (see 'Webster's sources and borrowings', p. 36) but what is interesting is the way in which he has interpreted and augmented these characters. Antonio is developed; Bosola emerges in a central role and his actions as a revenger in Act V are entirely Webster's invention, as is the fate of the two brothers; and the Duchess is much more complex than Belleforest's wanton widow.

The Duchess

The Duchess has been described as 'one of the great romantic heroines of English drama, impulsive, impatient of social proprieties, straightforward, warm, sensual and elegantly feminine' (J. Leeds Barroll: *The Revels History of English Drama*, Volume III 1576–1613, Methuen, London, 1975). We are first introduced to her in the second scene of the play by Antonio who, after describing her two brothers, speaks of her by way of contrast, extolling her virtues (I.2.109–31). We can accept this as an unbiased description; at this point in the play Antonio is merely a servant of the Duchess, with no thought of bridging the social chasm between them.

Yet even while her brothers are warning her against re-marriage, and she is responding calmly to their barely concealed menaces, the man whom she intends speedily to make her husband is waiting for her in the gallery (see I.2.132–280); and the determination with which she acts, doubly bold in that she is a woman wooing a man who is her social inferior, is the only way in which she resembles her brothers. Is her action merely impulsive? Is she marrying a man she scarcely knows? The construction of the first act of the play may make it look that way, but presumably Antonio, as her steward, is the member of her household with whom she would have worked most closely, and she would have had ample opportunity to assess his worth. This is apparent by the way she talks to him in the 'wooing' scene (see I.2.280 to the end of the scene). Certainly, she is of a generous and open-hearted disposition, and her fertility in quickly producing three children is a symbolic emphasis of this on the physical level. She is by no means the wanton woman as portrayed in some of the early versions of the story (see 'Webster's sources and borrowings', p. 36). It is an acute dramatic irony that in a relaxed bedroom scene of family intimacy, when all are off their guard – and indeed the Duchess jokes about just that (III.2.63) – it is at this moment that Ferdinand insinuates his way into her closet, overhears her speaking of her husband and children, and offers her a dagger with which to kill herself.

The straightforwardness of her and Antonio, for all their virtue, is clouded – even corrupted – by the evil world around them. Their integrity, initially blemished by the very need to keep their marriage a secret (although for the Duchess no marriage bonds could be stronger: see I.2.391–407), is further damaged by the necessity for a more open lie (III.2.166–74), despite the fact that the Duchess excuses it as 'a noble lie/'Cause it must shield our honours' (III.2.180–1). Furthermore, when Cariola protests that she does not like the idea of a bogus pilgrimage ('this jesting with religion') as a means of escape, the Duchess's dismissal of Cariola as a 'superstitious fool' strikes an ominous note (see III.2.306–20). Yet these taints seem as nothing when compared with the truly damnable offences committed against the Duchess and her family, and by her fortitude during her imprisonment and mental torture she becomes a great tragic figure of the English stage. When Ferdinand asks Bosola how she is behaving in her prison, that notable cynic replies that she displays 'a behaviour so noble,/As gives a majesty to adversity' (IV.1.5–6). The Duchess's warmth and life is such that shutting her away from the light is the worst that can be done to her, worse than torture or death itself. In her isolation she comes close to despair and to cursing the universe (IV.1.95–109); but, unlike King Lear, she does not curse and go mad, as Ferdinand apparently hoped she would, but rises above despair to an affirmation of self-respect: 'I am Duchess of Malfi still' (IV.2.139).

From this moment until her violent death, all she says is calm and positive. As Cariola is forced off-stage, the Duchess leaves domestic instructions about the care of her boy and girl in a way that may seem agonizingly pathetic to the audience, but which are not said with any sense of futility by the Duchess (has she – or has Webster – forgotten that she believes she has seen their dead bodies?). Even as she is about to be strangled, she commands: 'Pull, and pull strongly, for your able strength/Must pull down heaven upon me'; and she dies on her knees, in order to enter heaven humbly. After her death her echo persists (V.3); whereas the Cardinal is aware that after his death nothing shall remain (V.5.88–9).

Ferdinand and the Cardinal

Ferdinand and the Cardinal can be considered together as the unnatural brothers (the subtitle given to the fourth quarto of the play) who work together to bring about their sister's downfall and death. Bosola gives us his view of them right at the beginning of the play: 'He and his brother are like plum trees, that grow crooked over standing pools, they are rich, and o'erladen with fruit, but none but crows, pies, and caterpillars feed on them' (I.1.49–52). This contrasts with his apparently sincere view of Antonio as 'like a cedar, planted by a spring' (III.2.263). The Cardinal has a reputation for gambling, dancing, womanising and fighting duels, but it seems that he only does these things because he feels they are expected of him. Antonio gives a truer picture of his inward character as 'a melancholy churchman' and assures that 'some good he hath done' (see I.2.75–89); but there is no elaboration of this goodness anywhere in the play. Antonio goes on to describe the unstable character of Ferdinand, 'a most perverse and turbulent nature'. He is a Jacobean image of the Machievellian tyrant: he enjoys cunningly trapping malefactors and condemning them, and both brothers are surrounded by many flatterers (I.2.91–108). Yet in certain respects the two characters are contrasting, and nowhere is this better shown than in Act II Scene 5, after they have received the letter from Bosola which tells that their sister has had a child. Ferdinand is uncontrollable, almost manic; the Cardinal is cool and reasoning, threatening to leave unless Ferdinand calms himself. The persistent imagery of heat and cold in the play is embodied in the fire of Ferdinand and the ice of the Cardinal.

The cold ruthlessness of the Cardinal's character is evident in the way he disposes of Julia, his mistress, in Act V Scene 2. The Jacobean audience were used to Italian murderers using poison in ingenious ways (see 'The Italian setting', p. 35), but that a Cardinal should poison a Bible in order to dispose of his mistress when she kisses it epitomises the appalling amorality of this man of the Church. His guilty conscience is merely 'tedious'; the promptings of his mind concerning the operation of hell-fire seem to come from an academic interest; and his vision that out of his garden fishpond comes 'a thing arm'd with a rake/That seems to strike at me' is greeted with wonder rather than fear (V.5.1–8). Yet when Bosola comes to kill him he makes vain offers and cries out in panic, finally dying without dignity 'like a leveret' (V.5.44) and with a sudden awareness of his own insignificance: 'And now, I pray, let me/Be laid by, and never thought of' (V.5.88–9).

While the Cardinal's motives for hounding his sister appear mainly a question of family pride (see II.5.21–3), Ferdinand's motives are complex. Webster adds to the dark ambiguity of his nature by not allowing the spectator to decide quite what is in Ferdinand's mind, if indeed he knows himself (III.1.83–9). He claims, perhaps believes, that he hoped to gain materially by the Duchess's death (IV.2.275–80). Yet when he hears that she has had a child his imagination seethes, and in powerfully unpleasant imagery he imagines he sees his sister in the sexual act (II.5.43–6). He envisages a savage vengeance (II.5.67–74). If you follow up the last two references it can be seen that Ferdinand's language sounds more like that of a jealous lover rather than an angry brother who either hopes to gain treasure by the Duchess dying single or feels that his family honour has been wounded. After he has instructed her never again to undertake 'those joys/Those lustful pleasures' of the marriage bed, he makes a gratuitous reference to women's liking for 'that part, which, like the lamprey,/Hath nev'r a bone in't', pretending he refers to the tongue, and leaves her with 'Farewell, lusty widow' (see I.2.244–59): this is curious language from a brother to a sister, and seems charged with incestuous emotion.

For all his savage cruelty and eventual madness, Ferdinand is not without a certain self-awareness. He appreciates it when Bosola, unlike most, refuses to flatter him (III.1.82–93), and knows, when he confronts the Duchess in her bedchamber, that, if he were to discover who it is that has 'enjoy'd' his sister, his violent reaction would be uncontrollable (III.2.91–100). His unfeelingness is apparent in the imprisonment of his sister, the attempts to drive her to despair by surrounding her with mad folk, the giving to her of a dead man's hand to hold, and the display to her of wax figures of her husband and children appearing as if they were dead. Yet when Bosola brings to him her dead body, his response is stunned: 'Cover her face. Mine eyes dazzle: she di'd young.' A reaction quickly follows whereby he blames not himself but Bosola, the instrument of his villainy (IV.2.255–327). His anguished cry, 'I bad thee, when I was distracted of my wits,/Go kill my dearest friend, and thou hast done't', is reminiscent of the traditional reaction of Henry II towards the knights who killed Thomas Becket, and of Bolingbroke after Exton has murdered the deposed king in Shakespeare's *Richard II*. In his departing words of Act IV Scene 2, he sounds as if his wits are already turning: 'I'll go hunt the badger by owl-light:/'Tis a deed of darkness.' He degenerates into lycanthropia; is seen in graveyards at night carrying limbs from dead bodies; and finally, in a violent climax of madness, thinks that the Cardinal his brother is an enemy upon a battlefield and stabs him, stabs Bosola, and is himself struck down by the dying Bosola. He dies exposing his conscience in a single line: 'My sister, oh! my sister, there's the cause on't', leaving the spectator to ponder on the ambiguity of his motives toward her.

Antonio

The problem with Antonio is that he is so bland a character that it is difficult to see him in his own light. It is true that from his admiration of good practices in the French court and his shrewd yet compassionate assessment of Bosola in the first scene of the play, we receive a favourable impression of him; but principally he is seen to be most worthy because the Duchess sees him so. His balanced, sane views stand out in a corrupt world. His modesty, honesty and humility, and the Duchess's recognition of these qualities, can be seen in Act I Scene 2 after the Duchess has placed the ring upon his finger (see I.2.337–56). Here his language, stately and dignified, contrasts with the harsh ranting and lurid images of Ferdinand. Another good example of his temperament as expressed by his language is to be found towards the end of the play when viewing the ruins of an ancient abbey:

> I do love these ancient ruins:
> We never tread upon them, but we set
> Our foot upon some reverend history . . .
>
> (V.3.9–11)

And he continues in this vein in language that is measured yet just avoids pomposity.

For all his honesty, or rather because of it, he is well aware that he and the Duchess are being forced into deceit by the corruption around them. In order to prevent discovery that the Duchess is about to give birth, he gives out that jewels and plate have been stolen; confines all officers to their quarters on suspicion of the supposed theft; and then suggests to Bosola that he has poisoned the Duchess with the apricots which he gave her, having already instructed Delio to make public this false accusation. Although Antonio fears that the inquisitive Bosola will find out the truth ('This mole does undermine me' – II.3.14 – and 'This fellow will undo me' – II.3.29), he has no reason to suspect Bosola to be an enemy: hence he has moved from a slur on the officers of the Duchess's household to a specific allegation against an innocent man (it is a nice irony that Bosola is accused of one crime of which he is not guilty). These tactics may not seem dire within the context of a corrupt world, but for Antonio himself they are a fall from virtue:

> The great are like the base; nay, they are the same,
> When they seek shameful ways to avoid shame.
>
> (II.3.51–2)

His dignity in adversity and his earnest attempts to be reconciled to the Cardinal in Act V earn him sympathy; yet he appears naive and less intelligent than both the Duchess and Delio, who have come to recognise the brothers for what they are. Whereas the ritual that builds up to the Duchess's death makes it powerful and gives it tragic stature, the sudden violence of Antonio's death, casual mistake that it is, makes his lonely and despairing end pathetic and even ridiculous. The Duchess is the heroine of the play; but Antonio is not the hero.

Bosola

In many ways Bosola is the most interesting and complex character in the play, and many would argue that his personal tragedy is as great as that of the Duchess herself. He is a man who has in him the power to do good, as is recognised by Antonio at the end of Act I Scene 1; but in his attempts to gain advancement he has persistently sold his services to evil men and, in serving them with loyalty, like a good soldier, has himself become an agent of evil. Throughout the play he is a malcontent, a neglected man of thwarted ambition, and the Jacobean audience would have recognised his dramatic type as dangerous. Delio explains that Bosola's melancholy was originally brought on by excessive study when he was a scholar at Padua (III.3.40–6); but earlier in the play he has given a harsher picture of what Bosola has become over the years:

> Here comes Bosola
> The only court-gall: yet I observe his railing
> Is not for simple love of piety:
> Indeed he rails at those things which he wants,
> Would be as lecherous, covetous, or proud,
> Bloody, or envious, as any man,
> If he had means to be so.
>
> (I.1.22–8)

At the beginning of the play, Bosola has already committed murder for the Cardinal and as a result has served a sentence as a galley slave. When the Cardinal treats his return to court coolly and refuses to advance his fortunes, Bosola replies that he will 'thrive some way' (I.1.38); and his cynicism – or perhaps it is his true understanding of the world in which he finds himself – is such that when Ferdinand summons him and offers him gold, his immediate reaction is 'Whose throat must I cut?' (I.2.170). Ferdinand gains him employment as Master of the Duchess's horse, but his real task for his new master is to spy on the Duchess and inform on her if she shows favour towards any suitor. 'I am your creature,' he tells the Duke (I.2.208), at whose suggestion he sets about his business by playing up his reputation as a melancholy cynic in a way that fools Antonio (II.1.78–110). His behaviour is designed to put those in the Duchess's household off their guard in order to assist his attempts to glean all possible information. When he suspects that the Duchess is pregnant, he cunningly proffers her apricots as a way of finding out whether she has the kind of craving typical of a pregnant woman (Act II Scene 2). Ferdinand salutes Bosola's plain-speaking and refusal to flatter (III.1.82–93); and it is a fine dramatic irony that it is no trick but an honest, if cynical, opinion on Bosola's part that elicits the information for which he has been waiting: by defending Antonio's virtue (III.2.228–73), his praise so overjoys the Duchess that she impulsively accepts him as a friend and tells him that Antonio is her husband and father to three children by her. He cannot believe his luck (III.2.276). Yet at the very moment of success he hates what he is going to do and feels self-contempt: 'Oh, this base quality/Of intelligencer . . . men that paint weeds, to the life, are prais'd' (III.2.325–9).

When Ferdinand asks how the Duchess is bearing her imprisonment, Bosola shows that he can appreciate the dignity with which she suffers, and this is evident not only in what he says but in the measured pace and general tone of his speech (IV.1.3–14). He conducts the persecution and presides over the execution of the Duchess without savagery or malice; he is merely carrying out his duty loyally, a function which is often used as an excuse for atrocity. When he goes to Ferdinand for his reward after the Duchess and her children have been strangled, and he is spurned and offered no more than a pardon for what he has done, he at last understands the futility of his strivings:

> I stand like one
> That long hath tane a sweet and golden dream,
> I am angry with myself, now that I wake.
>
> (IV.2.317–19)

He can now sum up himself the immorality of his service to Ferdinand:

> I served your tyranny: and rather strove
> To satisfy yourself, than all the world:
> And though I loath'd the evil, yet I lov'd
> You that did counsel it: and rather sought
> To appear a true servant than an honest man.
>
> (IV.2.323–7)

In retrospect, he now feels that he 'would not change my peace of conscience/For all the wealth of Europe' (IV.2.334–5). But it is too late. The revival of the Duchess offers him the tantalising possibility that he may yet do some good and rehabilitate himself; but when she finally expires, so does Bosola's hope of salvation, and all that is left to him is to pursue a course of vengeance against those who have caused his 'dejection'. (The ethics of Revenge Drama dictated that when a revenger had killed, then he himself must die. The audience of the day would have recognised that even Shakespeare's Hamlet, a far less tainted revenger than Bosola, is doomed to die once he has drawn blood by killing Polonius; so much the more Bosola – if he is not already damned for crimes committed before the action of the play commences.)

Hence Act V, through Bosola's revenge, adopts the shape of a traditional *dénouement* to a Jacobean revenge tragedy. As a final irony of fate, Bosola, now trying to strike at the forces of evil, by mistake kills Antonio. 'The man I would have sav'd 'bove mine own life!' (V.4.52). Yet he is not now to be deflected from his purpose by promises of wealth (V.5.14–16) and, having received his own death-wound while ensuring the deaths of the Cardinal and Ferdinand, provides his own epitaph as one

That was an actor in the main of all,
Much 'gainst mine own good nature, yet i' th' end
Neglected.

(V.5.84–6)

Delio

Delio's role in the play is to act as a steadfast friend and confidant to Antonio, commenting on characters and action or eliciting such comments from Antonio. He has few positive characteristics of his own. More than once Antonio stresses that Delio is his main support, a friend in whom he places an absolute trust (see II.2.59–75 and V.1.74–6). In many ways Delio's relationship to Antonio is similar to that of Horatio to Hamlet in *Hamlet*, except that whereas Hamlet is Horatio's intellectual superior, Delio seems to understand Antonio's position better than Antonio does himself (see V.1.1–13, and V.3.27 to end of scene). As a morally wholesome character who has stood outside the main action of the play, Delio is left (like Richmond at the end of Shakespeare's *Richard III*) to sum up: he comments on 'this great ruin', encapsulates in memorable imagery the futility of fame, and emphasises the need for a reassertion of the moral order:

Integrity of life is fame's best friend,
Which nobly, beyond death, shall crown the end.   (V.5.119–20)

Julia, Cariola, and the old lady

Julia speaks in only three scenes in the play (II.4, V.1, and V.2). Her inclusion seems to be so that she should serve as a contrast to the Duchess. Compare Julia's advances to Bosola in Act V Scene 2 and the Duchess's to Antonio in Act I Scene 2: both speak out of passion, yet the Duchess proves constant in her love, whereas Julia is merely seen in the context of a wanton who is changing sexual partners. The Cardinal,

Delio and Pescara all treat her with a complete lack of respect. The Cardinal is cynical of her womanly wiles, and talks of her as of a well-trained falcon who owes him thanks (see II.4.1–36); later, when he is weary of her, she is his 'ling'ring consumption' (V.2.225). Delio's request – or virtual directive – that she should become his mistress is blunt, and this is notable in a character who is usually circumspect and polite (II.4.72–4). To Pescara she is simply a strumpet (V.1.26–52). Even her dead body is treated disrespectfully (V.2.306–17) compared with those of the Duchess and Cariola.

Cariola is the Duchess's waiting woman and acts as a confidante, giving the Duchess someone to whom she can express her thoughts. In this capacity Cariola resembles Delio's role towards Antonio. She does not like the idea of 'jesting with religion' (III.2.316), but this is probably, as the Duchess suggests, out of superstition rather than genuine religious sensibilities. She endures her imprisonment with optimism and bravery, her courage only failing at the very end where she struggles and tries every excuse to avoid her death. In this she contrasts with the serenity of the Duchess's approach to death – although the deaths themselves are equally violent.

The old lady is a target for Bosola's abuse, and serves to emphasise that beneath the painted face of the court there is decay and rottenness.

The courtiers

The minor courtiers, such as Forobosco, Silvio, Roderigo, and Grisolan, exist principally to give a feeling of court life. We only see the court assembled in Act I Scene 2, and it is manifest here that its main occupation is trivial conversation and pleasurable entertainment. Castruchio is a fool and a flatterer; as an old man and a cuckold he embodies physically the decadence of court life. The officers of the Duchess's household are well summed-up by Bosola as flatterers who cheerfully abandon a master when his luck is out (III.2.212–41). Malateste, whom at one time Ferdinand suggests to his sister as a husband for her, is effete and unworthy of the name of soldier (III.3.1–33). Only the Marquis of Pescara is honourable, and serves to show that such men do exist, even in a world of corruption, ruthlessness and violence. Delio tells us that pressure had been put on Pescara (presumably by Ferdinand and the Cardinal) to seize lands formally held by Antonio, an action 'Much 'gainst his noble nature' (V.1.7). When Pescara refuses to give part of the seized land to Delio, and then promptly gives the same to 'such a creature' as Julia, he appears to the audience in an unfavourable light: however, our view is quickly changed when he explains why it is fitting the land should go to a strumpet, and not to his friend Delio (see Act V Scene 1, particularly lines 37–59).

Imagery

What is an image? This question perplexes many students. They should be comforted to know that eminent critics disagree among themselves as to the answer. There are two main schools of thought:

(a) An image is a use of language which stimulates a *visual* image in the mind of the reader or listener;

(b) An image is a use of language which stimulates in the mind an impression of *any* of the five senses – touch, sound, smell and taste, as well as sight.

As to what particular use of language may evoke an image, critics are also divided. Here, there are again two main schools of thought:

(a) An image can be created only by figurative language, that is, similes or metaphors.

(b) An image can be created by an effective direct description which is not necessarily a simile or a metaphor.

The definitions preferred by the author of these Notes are both those indicated as (b) above. (For amplification of the above distinctions there is a good chapter entitled 'Imagery' in Patrick Murray's *Literary Criticism: a Glossary of Major Terms*, Longman, London, 1978.)

Where drama is concerned, a potential image can be present in the words which can only be fully realised in production; for example the set design and stage effects for, say, Act IV of *The Duchess of Malfi* may be chosen in order to give a framework for the verbal imagery of prison and confinement. Stage-directors sometimes call these possibilities by the name of 'sub-text'.

Imagery in *The Duchess of Malfi*

Webster was a painstaking dramatic poet. He may have lacked the range of Shakespeare's imagery, but he was capable of arresting single images and elaborate combinations of image. The language of *The Duchess of Malfi* conveys with great power a carefully worked-out series of related images, although there is a danger that the literary student of Webster can be over-impressed by certain patterns of language which an audience would be unlikely to notice. As can be seen from the detailed notes below, much of the imagery of the play is derived from a clash of stark opposites. Frequent mention of the physical world and the universe at large as a reflection of man, and vice versa, is typical of the kind of seventeenth-century poetry which became known as 'metaphysical'. The truth is evident of Clifford Leech's assertion: 'The imagery . . . is predominantly on the side of the play's destructive forces' (see the chapter on imagery in his book *Webster: The Duchess of Malfi*, Arnold, London, 1963).

Court life: corruption, disease and death

In the first two scenes of the play Webster does much more than introduce various characters: he establishes basic themes and images which run through the play. Often the images of corruption are associated with the court, and by making comments about behaviour in Italian palaces, Webster could satirise court life nearer home without seeming to be making a direct attack.

In the first scene of the play, Antonio takes an image common to both public square and palace courtyard, namely a fountain, and likens it to a prince's court:

> a Prince's court
> Is like a common fountain, whence should flow
> Pure silver-drops in general. But if't chance
> Some curs'd example poison't near the head,
> Death and diseases through the whole land spread.
>
> (I.1.11–15)

(Bosola, crying with remorse after he has murdered the Duchess, talks of his tears as 'penitent fountains' which were 'frozen up' while the Duchess was living.) The clear flowing fountain of the French king's court, as described by Antonio, is soon compared to the stagnant waters of the courts of the Duke Ferdinand and the Cardinal as perceived by Bosola:

> He and his brother are like plum trees, that grow crooked over standing pools, they are rich, and o'er laden with fruit, but none but crows, pies, and caterpillars feed on them.
>
> (I.1.49–52)

Yet he is happy enough to thrive by them if he can:

> Could I be one of their flatt'ring pandars, I would hang on their ears like a horse-leech, till I were full, and then drop off.
>
> (I.1.52–4)

He knows that his own corruption 'grew out of horse dung' (I.2.207–8) – as did the tempting apricots which the pregnant Duchess greedily eats (II.1.141–3). He even sees wisdom as a subtle cunning, describing it as 'a foul tetter, that runs all over a man's body' (II.1.80–1). The bodies of Castruchio and the old lady are a physical manifestation of the moral corruption and decay in the court. When Antonio falls from favour, Bosola comments sourly on the lice who fed upon his prosperity but who now drop off (III.2.235); and the Cardinal refers to his mistress, Julia, as 'my ling'ring consumption' (V.2.225) shortly before he poisons her, planning to give out that she died of the plague.

When the imprisoned Duchess asks in her anguish 'Who am I?', she is answered by Bosola's relentless analysis of the inevitable corruption of the body:

> Thou art a box of worm seed, at best, but a salvatory of green mummy: what's this flesh? a little cruded milk, fantastical puff-paste: our bodies are weaker than those paper prisons boys use to keep flies in: more contemptible; since ours is to preserve earth-worms . . .
>
> (IV.2.123–7)

The Duchess's ordeal culminates in an elaborate ritual of death, a *danse macabre* of mental torture followed by an almost ceremonial strangulation: for the end of all these images of corruption and disease can only be death. Images of coffins and tombs are frequent in the latter part of the play (for example, III.2.113–15; IV.2.145–74). Despite the fact that Antonio's comment on death and burial (V.3.9–19) elicits an echo ('from the Duchess' grave' say the stage directions), Bosola's nihilistic death-words at the end of the play remain the final comment:

> We are only like dead walls, or vaulted graves
> That, ruin'd, yields no echo.
>
> (V.5.96–7)

Appearance and reality

The difference between appearances and inner realities is a favourite theme of playwrights of the period, particularly Shakespeare. *The Duchess of Malfi* is full of allusions to this difference. When Bosola pretends to comfort the Duchess, she asks him: 'why dost thou wrap thy poison'd pills/In gold and sugar?' (IV.1.19–20). Later, Bosola himself shows that he sees through the smooth-speaking Cardinal: 'wherefore should you lay fair marble colours/Upon your rotten purposes to me?' (V.2.292–3) Bosola also taunts the old lady about the 'scurvy face physic' of women, who paint their faces in order to hide the ravages beneath (see II.1.23–37; see also Act III Scene 1 of *Hamlet*, where Hamlet expresses similar sentiments to Ophelia). Images of clothing are frequently used to signify deception or hide corruption. Again, it is the spy and arch-deceiver Bosola who is most aware:

> Though we are eaten up of lice, and worms,
> And though continually we bear about us
> A rotten and dead body, we delight
> To hide it in rich tissue.
>
> (II.1.58–61)

Ferdinand, instructing him how to spy effectively, suggests that as a cover Bosola keep his 'old garb of melancholy' (I.2.199). Later, when the Duke finds out that Antonio is the father of his sister's children, he sees a powerful double image of a fair exterior corrupted from within:

> Methinks her fault and beauty
> Blended together, show like leprosy,
> The whiter, the fouler.
>
> (III.3.61–3)

From Ferdinand, who, like Bosola, is so aware of the art of cunning, comes the supreme statement in the play concerning the falseness of the court:

> You live in a rank pasture here, i' th' court,
> There is a kind of honey-dew that's deadly:
> 'Twill poison your fame; look to't; be not cunning:
> For they whose faces do belie their hearts
> Are witches, ere they arrive at twenty years,
> Ay: and give the devil suck.
>
> (I.2.227–32)

Potential violence and menace

The actual moments of violence in the play are swiftly over: however, much of the imagery suggests a threat of violence which maintains tension and promotes an atmosphere of almost constant menace. Bosola describes a great man's treacherous followers thus:

> ... I have seen some,
> Feed in a lord's dish, half asleep, not seeming
> To listen to any talk: and yet these rogues
> Have cut his throat in a dream.
>
> (I.2.203–6)

Having found out about the Duchess's secret marriage, he comments upon his own stealth:

> A politician is the devil's quilted anvil,
> He fashions all sins on him, and the blows
> Are never heard.
>
> (III.2.321–3)

With a mixture of metaphor and simile, Julia says how, in order to squeeze information from the Cardinal, she will 'wind my tongue about his heart/Like a skein of silk' (V.2.219–20). Delio describes Ferdinand as 'Like a deadly cannon, that lightens ere it smokes' (III.3.54); and, at the moment of her betrayal, the Duchess sees herself as 'like to a rusty o'ercharged cannon' which could at any time 'fly in pieces' (III.5.102–3).

Nature and the cosmos

There are many allusions to natural phenomena in the play, and often they are images that suggest a universal upheaval of which the violence in the human world is a microcosm. Antonio describes the Cardinal as one who 'is so quiet, that he seems to sleep/The tempest out, as dormice do in winter' (III.1.21–2); and Silvio observes how he 'lifts up's nose, like a foul porpoise before a storm' (III.3.52). Likewise the Duchess sees Ferdinand as 'like to calm weather/At sea before a tempest' (III.5.24–5); although earlier, on Antonio's mention of the threat posed by her brothers, she is confident that, even if their marriage is discovered, 'time will easily/Scatter the tempest' (I.2.386–7).

There are many other images of harsh weather in the play. Some examples are: III.2.209–11 ('moisture/sea/foul weather'); III.3.59 ('sun/tempest'); I.2.163 ('shaking of the cedar tree'); V.5.93 ('mist'); V.5.114–5 ('frost/snow/sun').

More general images of nature also abound, for example: II.4.82 ('whirlpools'); II.5.79 ('scorpions'); III.2.86 ('bird's wings'); III.5.5–20 ('fledg'd buntings/pearls/tears/birds, that live i' th' field'); V.2.324 (planting of trust); V.5.5. ('fishponds').

Trees by water are used to symbolise the uprightness of Antonio:

... like a cedar, planted by a spring,
The spring bathes the tree's root, the grateful tree
Rewards it with his shadow

(III.2.263–5)

and the rottenness of the Aragonian brothers:

... like plum trees, that grow crooked over standing pools...

(I.1.49–50)

Many images operate on a more cosmic level, for example: I.2.169 ('thunderbolts'); II.5.80 and III.2.73 ('eclipse'). Having made the decision to court Antonio's love, the Duchess feels that she is 'going into a wilderness' (I.2.278). Later, she exclaims despairingly:

I could curse the stars ...
And those three smiling seasons of the year
Into a Russian winter: nay the world
To its first chaos.

(IV.1.95–8)

Bosola warns her that her pathetic perception of the universe does not affect reality, and coldly replies: 'Look you, the stars shine still' (IV.1.99). Ironically, it is Bosola, having killed the man he meant to save, who utters the pathetic fallacy: 'We are merely the stars' tennis-balls, struck and banded/Which way please them' (V.4.53–4). And presenting the bodies of the Duchess and her children to Ferdinand, he asks:

> Do not weep?
> Other sins only speak; murther shrieks out:
> The element of water moistens the earth,
> But blood flies upwards, and bedews the heavens.
>
> (IV.2.255–8)

Heat and cold: light and dark

A carefully-planned pattern of opposites, often of an extreme nature, is evident in the play. All the qualities of heat and cold, light and darkness are compressed by Bosola into a single image as he comments on the vanity of rank and fortune:

> Glories, like glow-worms, afar off shine bright,
> But look'd to near, have neither heat not light.
>
> (IV.2.141–2)

Later, in a striking paradox, he notes the hell that humans endure whereby, pursuing vain hopes, 'We seem to sweat in ice and freeze in fire' (IV.2.332). Markedly similar imagery occurs when Bosola tells Antonio 'Methinks 'tis very cold, and yet you sweat' (II.3.19) and when Ferdinand feels that had he been 'damn'd in hell', upon hearing of his sister's secret he would have been put 'Into a cold sweat' (II.5.75–7). The Cardinal more than once comments on the nature of hell-fire (V.2.303–5; V.5.1–3). The very characters of the two brothers are metaphors for heat (Ferdinand) and cold (the Cardinal – even his lust for Julia appears to be a cold thing). Antonio, sensible of the dangers inherent in accepting the elevation in fortunes offered by marriage to the Duchess, observes that:

>   he's a fool
> That, being a-cold, would thrust his hands i' th' fire
> To warm them.
>
> (I.2.343–5)

During her persecution the Duchess, thinking that she looks on the corpse of her husband, accounts it a mercy 'If they would bind me to that lifeless trunk,/And let me freeze to death' (IV.1.68–9); yet in the next scene she declares: 'Th'heaven o'er my head seems made of molten brass,/The earth of flaming sulphur, yet I am not mad' (IV.2.26–7).

Other images of cold are plentiful (for example, II.3.6; IV.2.358–60; V.2.328–9). In the last speech of the play Delio, commenting like Bosola on the vanity of fame, again combines extremes (V.5.112–16).

Images of light are mainly conveyed through cold hard words such as 'diamonds' or 'stars'. Antonio says at the beginning of the play that the Duchess 'lights the time to come' (I.2.131); it is ironic that Ferdinand should put her into such darkness when he visits her in his prison. Yet when he sees her dead, the full horror of it all makes his eyes 'dazzle' (IV.2.259).

Prison and confinement

There is much imagery which contrasts with the largeness of the universe and the freedom of nature. Such a contrast is embodied in the Duchess's words near the end of Act III, where she bemoans the constraints placed upon those of her rank:

> The birds, that live i' th' field
> On the wild benefit of nature, live
> Happier than we; for they may choose their mates,
> And carol their sweet pleasures to the spring.
>
> (III.5.17–20)

Early in the play the Cardinal warns the Duchess that 'The marriage night/Is the entrance into some prison' (I.2.243–4) – words that prove to be literally true. Images of nets or cages are frequent. Delio tells Antonio how Ferdinand, when he is acting as a judge, enjoys a trick of seeming 'to sleep o' th' bench/Only to entrap offenders in their answers.' And Delio replies:

> Then the law to him
> Is like a foul black cobweb to a spider,
> He makes it his dwelling, and a prison
> To entangle those shall feed him.
>
> (I.2.99–102)

Ferdinand himself talks of hypocrisy as Vulcan's engine, which was a net (see glossary to Act I Scene 2). Later Delio warns Antonio that the Aragonian brethren's letters of safe-conduct 'appear/But nets to entrap you.' (V.1.4–5). Bosola cites a caged lark as an image for the entrapment of the soul in the body, and Webster clearly intends it also as a metaphor for the cruel circumstances of the Duchess:

> didst thou ever see a lark in a cage? such is the soul in the body: this world is like her little turf of grass, and the heaven o'er our heads, like her looking-glass, only gives us a miserable knowledge of the small compass of our prison.
>
> (IV.2.127–31)

Much else contributes to a feeling of claustrophobia and constriction.

For instance: the Duchess asks why, she being a widow, her beauty should 'Be cas'd up, like a holy relic' (III.2.139); the First Pilgrim talks of the fall of Antonio as of one 'thrust into a well' (III.4.39); the Duchess warns against such of her retinue as remain with her all being caught together 'In one unlucky bottom' (III.5.58); and the Cardinal declares that those who are privy to a prince's secrets 'Had need have their breasts hoop'd with adamant/To contain them' (V.2.257–8).

Part 4

Hints for study

Preparing for an examination

In preparing for an examination you have probably read the play more than once; gone through it at least once in close detail, sometimes spending a whole session on the language, tone, character revelation, and other points of interest embodied in a single speech; and also, it is to be hoped, you have seen a performance of the play. The last is not always easy, since performances of a set play, other than Shakespeare, are rarely available when you want them. If you are lucky, however, and hear of a production of *The Duchess of Malfi*, even one for which you have to travel a distance, it is worth making the effort to see it. Even if it turns out to be an interpretation of the play which you think is wrong – perhaps particularly if this is the case – it is valuable because you are driven back to reviewing the text and testing your view of the play against that of the director and cast of the production you have seen. Also, you have been reminded that what you are studying is a piece of drama and not a book; and that its verse is dramatic verse, intended to be heard rather than read.

As the day of the examination draws closer, you will want to find ways of bringing your knowledge and understanding of the text to a peak, without driving out all freshness of response so that there is no enjoyment left in it for you. If this happens there is a danger that your essays in the examination will be dull and mechanical. Monotony can best be avoided by setting yourself varied tasks. Here are some suggestions:

(*a*) Spend some time reading through the entire play again, writing a series of symbols in the margin denoting different aspects of interest. For instance, you might write 'C' against words which illuminate facets of a Character, either the speaker or another; 'I' could be written in the margin alongside a distinctive piece of Imagery; 'T' adjacent to a notable Theme which runs through the play; 'IR' for IRony; and so on, inventing other symbols for any recurrent aspects of the play which you notice. When you have finished the play, make a list of references under different headings: this will help you to assemble your own thoughts and develop your own opinions.

(*b*) Commit to memory some useful *short* quotations – words, phrases, a few lines at most in each instance. You will find some useful ones used under various headings in Part 3 of these Notes.

(*c*) Write a paragraph summarising each act. Then try to summarise each act in two or three sentences. By comparing the two versions you can tell things about the dramatic structure. Which elements are vital? What have you left out in your second version and why? How much has the plot lost by your omissions?

(*d*) Ask somebody to start reading at random from the play: see how quickly you can identify the quotation, saying as much as you can about its context.

(*e*) Athletes train over the distance which they are going to run in competition: so should examinees. The examination will require you to answer a number of questions in a given time, and it is vital that you accustom yourself to this pressure. Find out how long you will have to write each essay in the examination. Then sit down in a quiet place, choose a title for a test essay, and do whatever reading and note-taking you think necessary by way of preparation. When you are ready, put all books and notes away, get out pen and paper, set an alarm clock for ten minutes less than your allotted time, and begin writing your essay (see (5) below under 'In an examination'). When the alarm rings, you have five minutes to draw the essay to a conclusion, and five minutes to check it through for mistakes. Leave the essay and come back to it later. How does it read? Did you say what you meant to? Did you leave out anything? Did you include anything which now seems irrelevant and better left out? Ask a teacher or lecturer to assess your essay if you can.

After a couple of attempts at this exercise, you may feel strong enough to write two essays consecutively. There is no point in this exercise unless you create examination room conditions for yourself. Write entirely uninterrupted: no background music and no getting up to make a cup of coffee in the middle!

In an examination

Here are some suggestions to help you in the examination room, in the order in which they may be considered:

(1) If there is a choice of question, consider carefully which will suit you best; but do not take too long to decide. Check how many questions you are required to answer on the paper as a whole.

(2) Read your chosen question carefully. If there are key words which you feel need clarifying, do that in the opening paragraph of your answer.

(3) If a question is in two parts, divide your time equally between each part, unless you can show in your answer why one aspect is more important than another.

(4) Answer the question asked. However good your ideas, they are worthless if misapplied. An art examiner was once asked: 'If a candidate is asked to paint an oak tree and he paints instead a perfect cedar tree, what is the painting worth?' The reply was 'Nothing'.

(5) Jot down a skeleton answer outlining the subject matter of each paragraph before you start to write the essay. As you write you may well find that new ideas emerge: be flexible and allow for these, departing from your plan if necessary. But if you start with no plan, then your essay will have no direction at any stage of its writing.

(6) Write legibly. An examiner probably has several hundred scripts to read: he will not be so well disposed towards a script which is very difficult to decipher.

(7) Keep your style clear and direct. Only use literary jargon when strictly appropriate; avoid impressive-sounding but long-winded and empty phraseology.

(8) Unless the question specifies an account, avoid narrative; use it only when necessary to illustrate your argument. Merely to tell the story as an answer to most questions is virtually worthless.

(9) Do not quote long passages. It is rare to find that more than two or three lines are relevant to any particular point, and it is painfully obvious to an examiner when a candidate has learnt a passage and is determined to fit it into his answer, whether or not it is pertinent to the argument in hand. (N.B. 'Quotation' is the noun – not 'quote', which is the verb.)

(10) There is no need to cite precise references. They are included in these Notes in order to help you to follow up and expand upon ideas. Wherever you can, indicate the act and scene of a reference or quotation; it will hardly be expected that you should have line references at your command.

(11) Refer to *The Duchess of Malfi* as 'the play' – never 'the book'.

(12) Never refer to a character as an 'actor'. While you should remember that you are dealing with a play, the term 'actor' refers to one who is playing the character, and not to the character him/herself.

(13) Only use a concluding paragraph if you have something more to say. You may wish to tie up some loose ends, or to assert a conclusion which you feel has not been sufficiently stressed; but it is a waste of time merely to repeat in summary what you have already said at length.

(14) Try to leave time to read through your answer, particularly if you know you are prone to make careless slips.

(15) The examination has a time limit. You should have worked out at the beginning how long you have for each question. Keep to your schedule as closely as possible. It helps if you ruthlessly omit unnecessary information, however tempted you may be to demonstrate to the examiner the range of your knowledge. If you do run short of time, resort to note form: display as much of your argument as possible, showing how the essay would have developed.

Model answers

In Part 3 of these Notes, under 'Characters' and 'Imagery', you will find sections which have been deliberately written as 'model' answers. They are acceptable answers (but see note 10 under 'In the examination') to the following questions:

(a) Write a detailed character study on any *one* of the following: The Duchess; Ferdinand; the Cardinal; Antonio; Bosola.

(b) Write an essay on the imagery of the play under any *one* of the following headings: Court life – corruption, disease and death; Appearance and reality; Potential violence and menace; Nature and the cosmos; Heat and cold – light and dark; Prison and confinement.

You will be lucky, however, if the questions in the examination are as straightforward as these. The following section will help you to use these Notes in a flexible way in order to tackle more complex questions than those above.

Guidelines for answers

If you use the guidelines below with discretion and not slavishly, following up the references given and combining them with your own responses and opinions, then you will be in a position to produce a good essay.

In the study of literature there is no such thing as a correct answer. Questions are asked in the spirit of debate and to see how well you can organise your ideas, and are not attempts to see if a candidate knows the 'right' answer. You should present all sides of an argument, and not merely the one which you favour. Give a structure to the way you display your knowledge and opinions, and *support what you say with close reference to the text*. Be disciplined: never allow yourself to get away with vague, general statements without referring to an appropriate part of the play in order to substantiate what you say. Quote where necessary – and remember that peppering your essay with single words or short phrases from the play in single quotation marks can be as effective as longer quotations. You should take the initiative and provide focus when a question is very general: this kind is usually more difficult than one on a specific aspect of the play, and it is easy to lose your way. The sections in Parts 1 and 3 of these Notes which are essentially background material (for example, 'The Italian setting') are intended to help you to understand the atmosphere of the play. The information therein should be used very sparingly in an essay, and should never be allowed to crowd out a close consideration of the text.

The questions below are in no particular order, any more than the examiner will choose to ask you one particular question rather than another. Some of the guidelines are quite full; others offer only pointers, leaving you to expand the argument. Having thought about a question, you may wish to follow the procedure set out in note (*e*) of 'Preparing for an examination', above.

Question (1): Compare (a) the characters of Ferdinand and the Cardinal and (b) their motives for the treatment of the Duchess.

Decide which part of the question carries more weight. Most of the material for (*a*) can be found under 'Ferdinand and the Cardinal' in Part 3 of these Notes. The same section will help with (*b*), but here you must be careful in your selection of material: keep it relevant to the question. The section 'Webster's World' in Part 3 may also help. See also question (2) below.

Question (2): How important is revenge as a theme in the play?

There are two revenges pursued in the play: (*a*) the combined revenges of Ferdinand and the Cardinal against the Duchess – some of the guidelines under question (1) above will help here; and (*b*) Bosola's revenge in Act V against Ferdinand and the Cardinal – remember that until that time, Bosola is merely the agent of the brothers' revenge rather than the revenger himself. If you know any other revenge plays of the period, brief comparison is permissible – but by no means essential; beware irrelevance.

Most of your essay will be on revenge as a theme; but you may feel that it is not the most important theme, in which case you may illustrate your point by referring to other themes – which should in any event be mentioned.

Question (3): What are the main themes of the play?

A less focused version of question (2). There is much to say and a danger of losing your way. Discipline is required here, and what comprise the main themes is much a matter of opinion. A possible list is:

(*a*) The particular tragedies of the Duchess, Bosola and Ferdinand
(*b*) Universal mortality

(c) The decadence of court life
(d) The futility of greatness
(e) Revenge

The above are not in a particular order, although they may serve as a skeleton plan for an essay. Would you deal with them in the order above? Would you add to the list?

Question (4): 'The Duchess is not an entirely innocent woman: by her sensual nature, and by her ignoring the codes of her age and marrying beneath her, she does much to bring about her own downfall.' How fair do you consider this statement?
This is essentially a character assessment, but keep the question in mind. See Part 3 of the Notes for a consideration of the Duchess. See also the notes on the other women in the play, especially Julia. See under 'Women, marriage and widowhood' and 'Webster's sources and borrowings'.

Question (5): Assess briefly the roles in the play of the following minor characters: Castruchio, Julia, Cariola, Pescara.
See character commentaries in Part 3.

Question (6): Discuss the way prose and verse is used in the play.
Take the section in Part 3 headed 'Verse and prose' as a starting point. One example is given there of the use of prose and verse: examine this passage more closely. In the light of general comments in this section, find other examples that will give substance to your essay.

Question (7): 'The imagery of death'. Consider the imagery of the play in the light of this epithet.
Use the section on 'Imagery' in Part 3. On first sight it may seem that the sub-section dealing with death contains most of the information you want. But does it? As with question (2) above there is an opportunity to suggest that the epithet in the title is an inadequate basis on which to consider the imagery of the play. This gives an opening to mention other kinds of imagery. However, it would be dodging the question if you dismissed too soon a discussion of 'the imagery of death' and concentrated on, say, 'the imagery of nature and the cosmos'; if you did this an examiner would probably conclude that you were deliberately twisting the question in order to write down a previously-prepared answer.

Question (8): 'Didst ever see a lark in a cage? Such is the soul in the body.' How far does this remark typify the imagery of the play?
See Part 3, 'Imagery', sub-section on 'Prison and confinement', but the same qualifications apply as for question (7) above.

Question (9): Is the plot of the play well-constructed?
See Part 3, the section headed 'The Dramatic Unities and structure'. Is it right to try to see the play as a well-shaped unit? Or is Webster trying for a different effect? Does he succeed?

Question (10): 'Webster's world is too fantastic and grotesque to have any effect on the modern audience.' Discuss.
See Part 3, the section 'Webster's world'. Then decide what you think.

Question (11): Discuss Webster's presentation of evil in the play.
This is a very open question – presentation of character, language and imagery, setting and atmosphere, plot structure, and general themes are all relevant; but do not be frightened of the question if you can say little under one or two of these headings and much under one or two others. It is quite fair, in a question like this, for you to declare an intention of focusing on what you see as the key issues – but you must justify your choice, and at least mention the range of issues in your opening paragraph. It is vital, again, that you make a skeleton plan, which could be something like this:
(a) Opening paragraph – declaration of intent in the essay.
(b) General atmosphere of the setting; tone of the court of Amalfi.
(c) Evil characters, and how the good are tainted by them (see Part 3, 'Characters').
(d) Language of evil – im.gery – this may well provide the bulk of your essay.

Question (12): 'The Duchess is not of sufficient moral stature for us to view her as truly tragic.' How far do you agree?
You should spot this as a variation of question (4).

Question (13): Consider the suggestion that it is Bosola who is the truly tragic figure in the play.
This question is not to be seen as requesting a mere character study. Before you start your essay, make a list of the ways in which Bosola is bad and the ways in which he is potentially good. Here, and in question (12) above, you need to think about what constitutes a tragedy, and what makes a character tragic.

Question (14): 'Webster was much possessed by death/And saw the skull beneath the skin.' (T. S. Eliot) Consider the play in the light of this statement.
Not exactly the same as question (7), although there is some overlap. As well as imagery, the themes of mortality and the vanity of human greatness need discussing.

Question (15): Is Act V an anti-climax?
The climax of the play can be seen as the death of the Duchess at the end

of Act IV. If anti-climax is to be avoided , then our interest must be successfully transferred to another character or other issues. Is it? Are Antonio's problems at the beginning of Act V a replacement for what we have lost? Does the play become a more conventional revenge play, with Bosola now fulfilling the role of revenger-hero? Is the final scene of multiple death convincing? The truth is that if the play is essentially about the Duchess, then there will be anti-climax; if it is more about the themes summed up in Delio's speech at the end of the play (V.5.109–20), then the play is not simply about one character, and you may feel that it sustains its dramatic tension to the end.

Model answer to question (15)

As early as Act I Scene 2 we feel that the Duchess is threatened. Her brothers try to browbeat her with warnings not to remarry, and as she prepares for her meeting with Antonio in order to confess her love to him, she senses that she is 'going into some wilderness'.

During Acts II and III, scenes of the Duchess, her family, and the court alternate with scenes concerning the activities of Ferdinand and the Cardinal, in such a way that our interest in the motives and actions of characters other than the Duchess – particularly Ferdinand and Bosola – are developed. Indeed, Bosola, who acts as a link between the two worlds, is established in his key role by the end of Act II.

Hence, when the Duchess is killed at the end of Act IV, there are other characters upon whom the audience can focus their attentions. In this world which is infected with evil, the spark of goodness has been extinguished with her death; and to maintain dramatic interest somebody has to take on the fight in Act V against the forces of evil. Antonio is too pale a character to fill this role; but Webster has well-prepared the ground during the first four acts, so that it is dramatically feasible for the rejected Bosola to regret his service as an agent of evil and to become a revenger-hero – or rather revenger-anti-hero – in Act V. Up to the end of Act IV he has only been the instrument for the brothers' vengeance. In Act V he becomes a revenger for his own cause: the power of Bosola's hatred creates in the spectator an expectation of a blood-soaked *dénouement*, and this anticipation does much to prevent a feeling of anti-climax after the Duchess's death.

It is true that while the action at the beginning of Act V dwells on Antonio's 'hope of reconcilement/to the Aragonian brethren', the action lacks interest; but then an anti-climax of some sort is inevitable after the events of Act IV, and Webster wisely picks up Antonio's story at this point in order to build up the tension from a low key as the act progresses. Many plays have an initial climax at the end of Act III (for example, the blinding of Gloucester in *King Lear*), and the playwright spends two acts building up to a final climax. Webster's achievement is that he does the same in one act. From Act V Scene 2 the action moves steadily towards the final catastrophe: Ferdinand's horrible madness has taken firm hold of him (there is a touch of humour here as the confident doctor fails to control his patient); Julia woos Bosola, acts as a spy for him, and is poisoned by the Cardinal; the action slows a little during the elegiac 'echo' scene (V.3); then Antonio is accidentally slain by Bosola (V.4); finally comes Bosola's revenge (V.5), by which the Cardinal and Ferdinand both die, and Bosola himself is fatally wounded. How convincing this last scene appears depends on the skill of the actors – and the same applies, of course, to the death of the Duchess: both scenes will be anti-climactic if not well-handled. Potentially, the end of the play is dramatically strong. Delio's final speech on the futile vanity of human greatness, a gentler version of Bosola's commentary to the Duchess before her death (IV.2.122–59), underlines a theme which has run through the play.

Relevant parts of the speech – V.5.108–20 – could be quoted here to round off the essay; this is a useful speech to learn.

Question (16): Discuss the use of irony in the play.
(See Part 3, 'Irony', for a general consideration of the word.) Most of the ironies in the play spring from misplaced confidence on the parts of the Duchess and Antonio. Some of the ironies are retrospective and would not necessarily be appreciated by a first-time audience who did not already know the play; for example, when the Duchess says to Antonio, as a marriage-pledge, 'I sign your *Quietus est*', it is only seen later that she is literally signing his death warrant (I.2.380). She does not fear her brothers' anger should they find out about Antonio and herself, declaring that 'should they know it, time will easily/Scatter the tempest' (I.2.386–7). When she asks blessing on her betrothal she says: 'Bless, Heaven, this sacred Gordian, which let violence/Never untwine' (I.2.393–4). But the anger of her brothers is to be long-lasting, leading to a very violent parting from her husband and the world. There are other little ironies in this scene: at the beginning we learn that Antonio is the best jouster in the Duchess's tournament and 'took the ring' most often (I.2.6); by line 332 he has taken another ring which is to prove more dangerous. When rumours are circulating about her, the Duchess is easily comforted by Ferdinand's assurances that he is deaf to them (III.1.46–56); this easy security continues in the following scene, which is relaxed and happy, full of domestic high spirits, with the Duchess even joking about the threat of her brothers at the very moment that Ferdinand is insinuating himself into her room (III.2.63).

Ironies surround Bosola. It is ironic that Antonio misunderstands the reasons for his melancholy (II.1.78–89); that Bosola gains the intelligence he seeks through honesty rather than cunning (see III.2.226 to end of scene); and that Bosola is fated to kill the one man he means well by (V.4.41 to end of scene).

On a larger scale, the theme of the vanity of human greatness can be brought into this essay (V.5.75–8 and 88–9). Bosola is well aware of the futility of princes' aspirations (IV.2.122–59). By the end of the play, the Duchess and her dignity, the Cardinal and his family honour, and 'the great Calabrian Duke' Ferdinand, are all reduced to 'these wretched eminent things' (V.5.112).

Question (17): A context question.
A context question is one where a passage from the play is printed, and you are asked one or more questions on the passage. If you are set one of these, remember that you must concentrate on the passage set, and may only discuss matters concerning the play as a whole if a question invites you to do so. An example of a context question might be as follows: IV.2.348–69 is printed out (Bosola's final speech of the scene). The questions that follow ask you: (i) What is the exact context of this passage? (ii) Explain what light this passage sheds on Bosola's character.

You may also be asked to explain briefly the meanings of certain words and phrases in the passage. Here, as with (i) above, there is no substitute for knowing the play thoroughly. Part (ii) must be answered with close reference to the passage, although it will be accepted that, in order to illustrate what light this passage sheds on Bosola, you must establish your view of Bosola up to this point in the play.

Part 5

Suggestions for further reading

The text

There are two good modern editions of *The Duchess of Malfi*: The Revels edition, edited by J. R. Brown, Methuen, London, 1964; and The New Mermaids edition, edited by Elizabeth M. Brennan, Benn, London, 1964. It is the latter edition which has been used in the compilation of these Notes, and to which all line references apply.

Other works by John Webster

Webster co-authored many plays, but there are only two other plays written by him alone: *The White Devil* (1612); and *The Devil's Law-Case* (*c*.1616). Another play, *Guise*, has been lost. It is recommended that students of *The Duchess of Malfi* should read *The White Devil*.

Criticism

It does not matter if you cannot obtain any of the books below. It is your reactions to the play that matter. In any event, get to know the play well first; only then will these critical works offer insights.

HOLDSWORTH, R. V. (ED.): *The White Devil and The Duchess of Malfi: A Casebook*, Casebook series, Macmillan, London, 1975.

HUNTER, G. K. and S. K. (EDS.): *John Webster*, Penguin Critical Anthology series, Penguin Books, Harmondsworth, 1969.

JUMP, JOHN D.: *The White Devil and The Duchess of Malfi*, Notes on English Literature series, Blackwell, Oxford, 1966.

LEECH, CLIFFORD: *John Webster: A Critical Study*, Hogarth Press, London, 1951.

LEECH, CLIFFORD: *Webster: The Duchess of Malfi* (Studies in English Literature No 8), Arnold, London, 1963.

MULRYNE, J. R.: *Jacobean Theatre* (Stratford-upon-Avon Studies, No 1), Arnold, London, 1960.

Background reading

LEEDS BARROLL, J.: *The Revels History of Drama in English, Volume III 1575–1613*, Methuen, London, 1975. See particularly pages 384 to 403 for 'the dark world of Jacobean tragedy'.

BOWERS, F. T.: *Elizabethan Revenge Tragedy 1587 to 1642*, Princeton University Press, Princeton, 1940.

BRADBROOK, M. C.: *Themes and Conventions of Elizabethan Tragedy*, Cambridge University Press, Cambridge, 1935.

BROOKE, RUPERT: *John Webster and the Elizabethan Drama*, Sidgwick & Jackson, London, 1916.

ELLIS-FERMOR, UNA: *The Jacobean Drama*, Methuen, London, 1936.

PROSSER, ELEANOR: *Hamlet and Revenge*, Stanford University Press, Stanford (California), 1967. Part One of this book concerns revenge tragedy in general, and is very useful.

The author of these notes

NEIL KING was educated at Sherborne School, and the Universities of Durham and Cambridge. He has taught in schools in Stockton-on-Tees, Watford, Bushey, and Cambridge, and has been an examiner in English Literature for five different examination boards. At present he is Senior English Master at Hymers College, Hull, and is engaged in research into aspects of moral and dramatic tension in Elizabethan and Jacobean Revenge Tragedy. He has written and co-authored plays which have been performed at Durham, Cambridge, and the Edinburgh International Festival.

The first 150 titles